LETTERS FROM THE END
OF THE WORLD

LETTERS FROM THE END OF THE WORLD

A Firsthand Account of the Bombing of Hiroshima

Toyofumi Ogura

Translated by
Kisaburo Murakami and Shigeru Fujii

KODANSHA INTERNATIONAL
Tokyo • New York • London

Originally published as *Zetsugo no kiroku* by Chuosha in 1948, and in paperback by Chuokoronsha in 1982.

Map on pages 12–13 by Keiichi Ogata.

Distributed in the United States by Kodansha America, Inc., and in the United Kingdom and continental Europe by Kodansha Europe Ltd.

Published by Kodansha International Ltd., 17–14 Otowa 1-chome, Bunkyo-ku, Tokyo 112–8652, and Kodansha America, Inc.

ISBN-13: 978-4-7700-2776-4
ISBN-10: 4-7700-2776-1

First edition, 1997
First paperback edition, 2001
15 14 13 12 11 10 09 08 07 06   10 9 8 7 6 5 4 3 2

Library of Congress Cataloging-in-Publication Data available

www.kodansha-intl.com

From "A Paper Grave"

—Toyofumi Ogura

Think of this book as a grave.
Not just one cold stone on the earth over you
but countless paper graves
flung to the far corners of the earth.
This way, it's lighter.

Contents

Preface

The atomic bombing of Hiroshima on August 6, 1945 was an event completely without precedent. As someone who was fortunate enough to survive that cataclysm, I felt at the time that firsthand accounts should be published as soon as possible, before people's memories could become clouded with the passage of time. But none appeared during the first or even the second year. However, toward the beginning of the third year, Mr. Yoshiro Sawamoto, who was then the president of Chuo-sha Publishing, suggested that I write an account of my experience. But this was not possible at the time: I was still teaching at the university, which had been almost totally destroyed, and as the only surviving member of our department still able to work, I needed to devote all my energy to helping to get the university going again.

But in my spare time, despite my lack of scientific knowledge of the bomb or the diseases associated with it, I had kept notes on the things I'd seen and heard in Hiroshima. These were recorded in odd notebooks, in the form of a series of letters to my wife, who had died from radiation sickness several weeks after the bombing. During that first year in particular, I had been seized with the desire to inform her of the events leading up to and following her death.

In response to Mr. Sawamoto's suggestion, I went over my notes. After taking out parts that were simply too personal and checking a few facts in newspapers and other sources, I hurriedly transcribed my notes onto manuscript paper, without any substantial rewriting or editing, and sent the manuscript to Mr. Sawamoto under the title, "Letters to My Departed Wife: Memoirs of the Atomic Bombing of Hiroshima." I only numbered the letters; he added the chapter titles later. My poet friend Kotaro Takamura tactfully described my prose as "simple and unsophisticated." His response no doubt stemmed largely from the clumsiness of my style, but the haste with which the manuscript was compiled may have had something to do with it too.

Mr. Sawamoto took the manuscript to the General Headquarters of the Allied forces in Japan (GHQ), for the censoring required of all Japanese publications during the Occupation. He was asked to make some modifications but they were all very minor, and the first edition came out not long afterward, in November 1948. The book went through six or seven printings in just six months, probably because it was the first eyewitness account of an atomic bombing ever to appear. They say it was also widely circulated among the Japanese populations of Hawaii and North and South America. The phrase "Printed in occupied Japan" was stamped on the back cover of copies intended for distribution overseas, and it remains etched in my mind to this day.

Hiroshima and Nagasaki are the only cities in the world ever to have been obliterated by atomic bombs. I understand that the bomb dropped on Hiroshima is now obsolete and would look like a child's toy if compared to the nuclear weapons available today. It is my hope that this book may suggest something of the horrors of the use of this weapon.

The reader will notice, though, that I do not offer any criticism of the American government for its decision to drop the bomb. This is not because of any deletions required by the censors; in fact, I made no such criticism. I've always believed that the use of this weapon was brought upon the country by the wartime leaders of imperial Japan, particularly the militarists who manipulated the emperor like a puppet and exploited the people for their own selfish ends. As a teacher at a national university, I had no choice but to comply reluctantly with the dictates of the government, even while despising myself for my own powerlessness. That the GHQ required only very minor modifications to my manuscript is no doubt the direct result of my abhorrence of Japan's wartime authorities.

Toyofumi Ogura
May 1982

		Direction and kilometers from hypocenter
Atagocho	①	E2.5
Danbara	②	SEE2.5
Dobashi	③	W0.5
Eba	④	SW3.0
Fuchu	⑤	E5.0
Fujimicho	⑥	SE1.0
Fukuromachi	⑦	SE0.5
Fukushimacho	⑧	W2.0
Funairi	⑨	SSW2.0
Funakoshi	⑩	SEE6.0
Furue	⑪	W4.0
Hakushima	⑫	NE2.0
Hatchobori	⑬	E1.0
Hirosecho	⑭	NW1.0
Inaricho	⑮	E1.5
Jigozen	⑯	SW15.0
Jisenjibana	⑰	HC Area
Kakocho	⑱	SSW1.5
Kamiyacho	⑲	HC Area
Kanayacho	⑳	E2.0
Kan'on	㉑	SWW2.0
Koi	㉒	W3.0
Kojincho	㉓	E2.0
Kusatsu	㉔	SWW5.0
Kusunokicho	㉕	N2.0
Kyukencho	㉖	NE2.0
Matoba	㉗	E2.0
Minamicho	㉘	SE3.0
Misasa	㉙	N2.0
Motomachi	㉚	HC Area
Mukaimada	㉛	SEE5.5
Nagaregawa	㉜	E1.0
Nakahirocho	㉝	NW1.5
Nigitsu	㉞	NE2.0
Noboricho	㉟	E1.0
Ogochi	㊱	NWW2.0
Ochigodao	㊲	NEE4.0
Onko	㊳	SE3.5
Osu	㊴	E4.5
Otemachi	㊵	HC Area
Onagacho	㊶	E3.0
Ozu	㊷	SEE3.5
Ozuguchi	㊸	SEE2.5
Sakaicho	㊹	W0.5
Sendamachi	㊺	S2.0
Takanohashi	㊻	S1.5
Takasu	㊼	W3.5
Takeyacho	㊽	SSE1.5
Teramachi	㊾	NW0.5
Uchikoshicho	㊿	NNW2.0
Ushida	�51	NE2.5
Ujina	�52	SSE4.0
Yamatecho	�53	NNW2.5
Yokogawa	�54	NNW1.5
Yoshijima	�55	SSW2.5

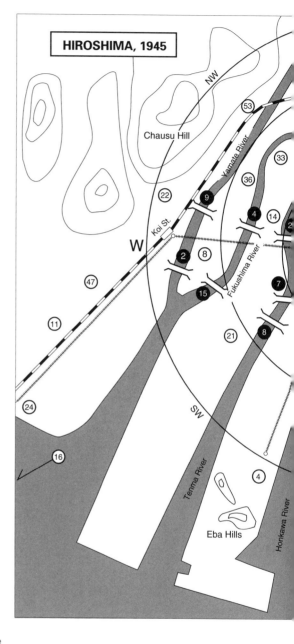

HIROSHIMA, 1945

❶ Aioi Bridge	⑫ Misasa Bridge
❷ Asahi Bridge	⑬ Miyuki Bridge
❸ Enko Bridge	⑭ Motoyasu Bridge
❹ Fukushima Bridge	⑮ Nishi-ohashi Bridge
❺ Higashi-ohashi Bridge	⑯ Sakae Bridge
❻ Hijiyama Bridge	⑰ Shin'ozu Bridge
❼ Honkawa Bridge	⑱ Sumiyoshi Bridge
❽ Kan'on Bridge	⑲ Taisho Bridge
❾ Koi Bridge	⑳ Tenma Bridge
❿ Kyobashi Bridge	㉑ Tokiwa Bridge
⓫ Meiji Bridge	㉒ Tsurumi Bridge

The last photograph taken of the entire family, spring 1945. (Clockwise from top left: the author, Toyofumi Ogura, aged 45; Kinji, 7; Fumiyo Ogura, 36; Keiichi 9; and Kazuko, 11.)

A Pageant of Clouds and Light

August 6, 1945

"'That was a huge lightning bolt!' I thought. Then I lost consciousness. This was in front of the Fukuya department store."

Fumiyo,

That was what you said, the words coming out in broken phrases, when I finally found you alive on the night of August 7. On the morning of the sixth, when you were standing at Hatchobori in front of Fukuya's, I happened to be near Mukainada, walking toward the city of Hiroshima.

It was a fine morning, windless and sultry, typical for the area around Hiroshima, as you know. The midsummer morning sunlight filled the sky to the point of overflowing. The brilliance of the light glinting off the mist in the blue sky was almost painful. The air-raid alert had been lifted about thirty minutes or an hour before and I was walking absentmindedly along the dusty paved road. I came to the east side of Shin'ozu Bridge. I stopped there for a minute, and just as I looked toward the sea and noticed the way the waves were sparkling, I saw, or rather felt, an enormous bluish white flash of light, as when a photographer lights a dish of magnesium. Off to my right, the sky split open over the city of Hiroshima. I instinctively flung myself facedown onto the ground.

I lay there without moving. Then I raised my head and looked up over the city. To the west, in the sky that had been blue a

15

minute before, I saw a mass of white clouds—or was it smoke? Whichever it was, it had taken shape in an instant. Then a halo of sparkling lights, a little bit like the ring that forms around the moon as a sign of rain, appeared near the cloud mass and expanded like a rainbow. The outer edges of the white cloud mass rolled down and curled inward toward the center while the entire shape ballooned out to the sides.

Immediately another mountain of clouds, accompanied by a huge column of red flame like lava from a volcano that had erupted in midair, formed under the first cloud mass. I don't know how to describe it. A massive cloud column defying all description appeared, boiling violently and seething upward. It was so big it blotted out much of the blue sky. Then the top of it began to spill down, like the breakup of some vast thundercloud, and the whole thing started to seep out and spread to the sides. The first cloud mass set down a foot like a huge waterspout, suddenly growing into the form of a monstrous mushroom. The two immense masses of clouds, one above the other, then rapidly formed into a single vast column of vapor, reaching all the way to the ground. Its shape was constantly changing and its colors were kaleidoscopic. Here and there it glittered with some small explosion.

I thought that it must be a manifestation of the *shumisen* cosmos that is supposed to exist at an astronomical distance from the earth, the one that the ancient Buddhists of India talked about. But the drawings of *shumisen*, as I recalled them to mind, paled into insignificance. I tried to visualize the cloud pillar seen by Moses that is mentioned in the Old Testament, but I couldn't. The unsophisticated concepts and fantasies dreamed up by the ancients were useless to describe this horrible pageant of clouds and lights staged in the firmament.

For a moment, I was in a trance, struck dumb. But the reality of the war that was in progress soon jolted me back to awareness. I tried to remember what little I had previously read or heard about bombs and other weapons. It couldn't have been flares at this time of day, I said to myself. I was sure it was neither incendiaries nor conventional bombs. In any case, I didn't see any aircraft. What was that flash of light? Those clouds? Maybe it was some kind of flame projection, or a death ray?

At the thought of a "death ray," my body tensed as if electricity had suddenly surged through it. Though I had heard the phrase before, I had no idea what it actually meant. I was filled with dread.

I glanced at my watch. It was just past 8:15 a.m. Just then there was a dull but tremendous roar as a crushing blast of air pressure assailed me.

I kept still, stretched out flat on the ground. At the moment of the roar and the blast, I had heard tremendous ripping, slamming and crashing sounds as houses and buildings were torn apart. I also thought I had heard screams. But these may simply have drifted into my memory later, or been products of my imagination.

However, I definitely did hear people crying afterward, "What's that?" "What happened?" And I saw people rushing from their houses out into the streets. I got up and looked around. I didn't see any houses in ruins then, nor any fires. I only saw figures running into the street. From where I stood at the foot of Shin'ozu Bridge, a wide road led right toward the city of Hiroshima. There were only a few houses nearby, at either end of the bridge. So it was easy for me to see people scattering like ants from a hill that had been kicked aside.

My thoughts were racing as a half-buried memory rose to mind: a roaring sound and a huge blast; a flash of light and ballooning clouds. An ammunition depot explosion!

That's it! I'd forgotten how many years before they had occurred, but I recalled cases of depots exploding in Hirakata in Osaka Prefecture and in Uji in Kyoto Prefecture.

An explosion in an ammunition depot! That's what it must have been, I thought. But the explosion was near the army's West Parade Ground. Was there an ammunition depot over there?

Like most people, I knew almost nothing about military matters. For all I knew, there could have been one underground, right in the middle of the city.

I looked up at the pageant of clouds and started thinking back on the horror stories I had heard about the explosions at Hirakata and Uji.

Just then, I heard excited voices.

"What do you think that is?"

"Where would that be?"

I turned and saw two men, both of medium build and around sixty years old, who looked like farmers.

"I guess it must have been near the West Parade Ground," I said.

"Yes, I think so too," one of the men responded.

"Was it a bomb?"

"No ..."

I held back, thinking I shouldn't make rash comments. As you know, the authorities were trying to control the spread of rumors. You couldn't blame them. For much of the war, Hiroshima had been spared the ravages of large-scale air raids, while other major cities were devastated one after another. Later I heard from an ex-army staff member that the army had suspected that the reason for this was that a number of enemy spies had infiltrated the city.

But their questions kept coming. One asked, "Was it some new kind of weapon?"

I responded, after a moment, "I think it was an ammunition depot exploding."

One of them said, "Do you suppose it was bombed?"

I actually imagined that the explosion had been caused by some bungling on the part of the army because it's impossible for bombs to fall when there is not a single airplane in the sky.

"You can't drop bombs without planes, you know," I replied, with a touch of sarcasm.

To my surprise, both men exclaimed, practically in unison, "Sure, but some planes did fly over!* From over there, heading that way." They pointed from the east toward the west.

---

* [Three B-29 bombers participated in the atomic bombing; one of them actually dropped the bomb.]

"When?" I demanded.

"A little while ago. They were B-29s."

Before I knew what to say, one of them cried out, "Hey! Aren't those parachutes?"

"Where?" I asked, looking in the direction he was pointing.

They were parachutes, all right. Three of them! Drifting along in a row, slightly aslant and off to the right of the monstrous cloud, were three white parachutes.

I was becoming confused. "You're right," I admitted. "But was there a crash?" It was rare for antiaircraft guns to hit their targets and, anyway, I hadn't heard any guns being fired. And the United States didn't engage in suicide bombing attacks like we did. Why would a crew abandon a plane if it weren't in trouble?

The two men said they hadn't seen any planes falling from the sky.

"That's odd," I remarked.

"We were watching the whole time," they insisted.

I was now completely at a loss. "Not being a soldier, I don't know what happened, but judging from the cloud and the noise, I'd say it was an ammunition depot blowing up," I said with bad grace, trying to hold my ground. Without arguing any further, the men politely thanked me and hurried off in the direction of Hiroshima. Now I had lost all confidence. I looked up again at the sky to the west. The three parachutes were still wafting in a northerly direction at an almost irritatingly constant speed.

I needed to think. It seemed clear that several planes, non-Japanese in origin, had flown over. Had they had some kind of mechanical trouble? That might explain the initial flash and the white cloud. The parachutes could have been opened by crew members who had bailed out. The smoke on the ground, the roaring sound and the explosive blast could all have been caused by an ammunition depot explosion. The planes could have dropped a bomb on a depot before they ran into some sort of trouble. That seemed almost plausible, though it would not explain the scale of the explosion. Perhaps this was some kind of new weapon, after all. Yet the ammunition depot explosion theory was hard for me to abandon, and I clung to it.

I learned later that I was not the only one who came up with a mistaken explanation. There were a lot of proponents of the "death ray" theory. A naval officer told some people that the explosion had been caused by an "aerial mine." I heard that theories about an ammunition depot explosion, a gas tank explosion or a fuel storage depot fire were popular not only among laymen but also with a considerable number of so-called "experts." It seems I was in good company.

The most absurd speculations centered on the parachutes. All the other theories proved to be short-lived; they were resolved in a matter of days. But stories about the parachutes continued to circulate in Japan, or perhaps I should say the world, for about seven to ten days after the event. And they were presented not as rumors or subjective, eyewitness accounts, but as official reports.

News of the bombing first appeared in the newspapers two days later, on August 8. Although I believe that radio stations did broadcast the story on the seventh, the situation in Hiroshima was such that no one was listening to the radio. The newspapers on the eighth mentioned "a new type of bomb." As far as I know, the phrase "atomic bomb" was used publicly for the first time in a speech by Prime Minister Suzuki after the broadcast on August 15 of the imperial rescript announcing Japan's unconditional surrender.

The main topic of speculation was the relationship between this "new type of bomb" and the parachutes. If I remember correctly, the topic first appeared in the papers on August 8. The article said that the new bomb was dropped by parachute and that it exploded in midair. I didn't think much about it at the time. But around August 12 or 13, the newspapers again explicitly mentioned "bombs attached to parachutes," and noted that the Osaka Air Defense Headquarters had issued "countermeasures" advising people that "the new-style, special bomb is attached to a parachute, so if you see a parachute falling, run to an air-raid shelter right away and lie facedown on the ground." This was so ridiculous it made me want to laugh.

The Japanese thus revealed to the rest of the world the state of panic and confusion into which they were thrown by the bombing, as well as their complete loss of common sense and the inadequacy of their powers of scientific observation and reasoning.

As I said, this was a new type of bomb that explodes with terrific violence in a fraction of a second. If such a bomb were attached to a parachute, it would be impossible for the parachute to survive, let alone descend in such an elegant manner. And when I saw the parachutes, they were nowhere near the source of the explosion. I thought this right from the start. I saw it with my own eyes.

I found out later from the newspapers that the parachutes we saw had been dropped at the same time as the bomb, from different planes. The parachutes carried radio-operated instruments for automatically measuring blast pressure and similar data that could then be transmitted back to the bombers' home base. I understand that this transmission was successfully completed, and that the parachutes were found lying in the hills of Kameyama northwest of Kabe. They had drifted a total of fourteen or fifteen kilometers. I also learned later that President Truman's international broadcast on August 6 announcing that an atomic bomb had just been dropped on Hiroshima was made immediately after the U.S. reception of the transmission from the parachute-borne instruments.

I was mulling over my theory of an ammunition dump explosion when my thoughts were interrupted by a truck crossing the bridge in the direction of Hiroshima. I looked back then and saw that others were approaching. There were three altogether, headed for the city, leaving behind a smell of exhaust and the shrill shouts of the people on board.

It looked like they were rescue squads on their way to Hiroshima.

My efforts to recall what little I knew of air raids left me with a crippling sense of insecurity. I could see that whatever this was, it was very bad. I thought I had better go over to Aiko's place and see how they were.

The home of your younger sister, Aiko Tateishi, was not too far—a kilometer or so—from where I was standing. Tightening the strap of the helmet I was wearing, I started walking or, rather, almost running.

Crowds of people were standing in front of their houses, gazing absentmindedly at the sky to the west. Many others were crawling out from the air-raid shelters that were everywhere in the narrow back streets.

The silence was thick and oppressive. Then a woman stuck her head out hesitantly from one shelter and shouted, "What happened?"

Someone answered in a frightened voice, "It's in the city!"

But as I got closer to the city, where rows of houses stood on either side of the streets, it became far noisier. People were moving about restlessly and no one was just standing around, dazed.

I spotted a man who was wearing only an undershirt and coming hurriedly out from a small side gate with a latticed door of the style you only see around Hiroshima. He was carrying someone piggyback, a woman. Her short white summer dress was stained red with blood, from the shoulder to the sleeve. Blood was pouring from her head and from her arm. The man was apparently trying to take her to a doctor. After they passed by, I saw a young woman wearing the same sort of summer clothing, carrying a man on her back. She was coming quickly toward me. The man was dressed only in underwear, and his face and upper torso were covered with blood.

"What happened?" I asked almost involuntarily.

"Glass," the woman said as she hurried past.

Must have been from the blast of air, I thought as I walked on, glancing at the houses on either side of the street. There didn't seem to be much destruction there, which I found strange. Later I realized that the area was about four kilometers from the center of the explosion, which meant that the destruction of roof tiles and windowpanes should have been fairly extensive, but that since the streets ran east–west, the rows of houses stood parallel to the direction of the blast, which minimized the destruction to the facades. But there must have been considerable damage to the walls and the fixtures on the west sides of the houses. So the injured people I had seen must have been hurt by flying fragments of glass from windows and doors that faced west.

I suddenly noticed I was walking right down the middle of the street. I veered over toward the left, much closer to the edge. As I walked along, practically under the eaves of the houses, I could hear the commotion going on inside.

"Where are the bandages?"

"Bring the first-aid box, quick!"

"Mother!"

"It hurts!"

Children crying, men shouting, noises that sounded like pieces of furniture being kicked, clomping sounds of feet running down stairs … This jumble of sounds gave a hint as to the chaos that must have prevailed in each house.

The number of people coming from the city gradually increased. Most were shuffling slowly along, dejection on their faces. They didn't appear to have any injuries, yet in many cases their clothing was ragged and scorched. One woman had one leg of her *monpe* work trousers torn off. Some people were barefoot.

Then I spotted, running toward me, a woman wearing a pair of work trousers and a single *geta* clog. She kept her head down and was covering the side of her face with one hand.

"What happened to you?" I called out.

"The bomb …" she said.

"Where was this?"

"At Kojin," she replied.

The woman went on past. Now a man approached, pushing a bicycle with bent handlebars; it looked as if he'd been in a crash.

"A bomb?" I asked.

"Yes, at Danbara," he replied. "My bicycle was picked right up off the ground and slammed back down."

The bike didn't seem to move very smoothly. I was becoming more puzzled all the time. Anyway, I could see I had better get over to Aiko's quickly. I started running.

I learned later that almost everyone in the city who survived the blast thought that a bomb had gone off right next to them. A lot of people who were inside at the time thought that their own houses had been directly hit. So when they were asked where the bomb had fallen, everyone would name the spot where he or she was at the time of the explosion. That would explain what the woman and man I mentioned had said. I also learned that at distances of three kilometers or so from the center of the explosion, people who were not in some way shielded from the bright flash of light received burns from the heat rays on any portions of their skin that were exposed. Many had their clothes scorched by the heat or ripped apart by the force of the blast.

The area where I was walking at the time was about four kilometers from the center of the explosion. If I had been just a little closer to Hiroshima, I wouldn't have escaped being burned myself. At the time though, I was completely unaware of this.

In any case, the magnitude of what had happened in that instant was of course far beyond my imagination. I only learned all this afterwards.

They say that the flash and the pageant of clouds were visible even from a distance of one hundred kilometers, that the thunderous roar could be heard at eighty kilometers and the force of the blast felt at sixty.

It was reported that glass in the doors and windowpanes of buildings thirteen and fourteen kilometers away was shattered. Indeed, all the windowpanes facing east at your sister Setsuko's house in Jigozen, a good fifteen kilometers to the southwest, were broken. I also heard that some windowpanes on even the island of Miyajima, a little further still, had been broken.

—November 10, 1945

A Blast and a Wave of Heat

August 6, 1945

Fumiyo,

Today I will tell you what happened to your sister, Aiko—who I know was your favorite—and her husband's family, the Tateishis, that day.

I think it was past nine o'clock, maybe even closer to ten, when I finally arrived at their house.

It was at the western edge of Ozucho, of course. The new road I had taken to get there came to an end just in front of their house. Construction was not yet completed on the portion from there to the city. So the road veered abruptly to the left just in front of the house, running into the narrow old road for a while, then forking into the road along the left bank of the Enko River and the one coming from the Higashi-ohashi Bridge. Even in normal circumstances, the old road was dangerously congested with trucks and buses.

The number of trucks on it—and the congestion—were appalling. This is because the road from Hiroshima and the one from Kure, where a naval base was located and which had been only partially paralyzed by bombings, came together at that point to form a vital link in the only system of road transportation available. Trucks coming into and leaving Hiroshima had brought traffic nearly to a standstill.

In the midst of all this congestion, droves of civilian victims of the bombing, most in a shocked stupor, came walking along, oblivious to the honking of horns and the curses of truck drivers. I had to weave my way through to get to the front of the Tateishis' house-cum-shop.

The house was still standing but there wasn't a pane of glass left intact in the sliding front door or display window. Only a few shards were wedged in the frame. The pavement under my feet was covered with broken glass, fragments of roof tiles, large pieces of plaster and so on. The slightest step made a crunching sound underfoot.

I forced the badly bent door to slide open, pulled aside the curtain, and tried to enter the shop, but a big, toppled-over display case blocked my way. I finally managed to get into the shop by crawling under the case.

I called out but there was no answer. I shouted out louder but was greeted with silence. Looking around inside the shop, I saw a dislocated beam hanging down from the ceiling. The west wall had a big hole in it up toward the ceiling, through which the damaged wall and roof of the house next door could be seen. A chest of drawers and a dressing mirror lay overturned in the living room. Thinking that there might be someone upstairs, I approached the foot of the stairs and looked up, only to be dazzled by the bright blue sky. There was a large hole in the roof and boards were hanging loosely from the ceiling. The steps were littered with clay and plaster from the walls, fragments of roof tiles and pieces of broken lumber.

I shouted loudly again but got no reply. I could see part of the sunny backyard through the back door of the living room, which was standing open. The Tateishis' air-raid shelter had to be out there somewhere. Just then I thought I heard voices. So I went outside again and proceeded through the narrow alleyway on the left side of the house to the back. The detached house in back, which they rented out, looked intact from the outside, but inside, the destruction was as bad as in Aiko's house.

I was amazed all over again by the extent of the destruction in

Aiko's house when I saw it a second time. The blast had opened a big hole in the tiled roof. The tiles were all cracked, missing or dislodged. All the ceiling boards upstairs had been ripped off. The west wall must have collapsed and allowed the force of the blast to storm right through the shop and the living room downstairs. A framed picture that had probably been hanging on the wall was now lying on the floor, and shelves were overturned. The blast had thrown sliding doors off their runners, penetrated into closets and even wreaked havoc with a small shoe cabinet, scattering its contents. Bookshelves were lying on their sides, and the books were strewn all over. A cooking pot from the kitchen adorned the alcove; the miniature family Shinto altar was now enshrined on the bathroom floor. Such farcical scenes were apparently not unique to this house. Later it turned out that everyone had similar stories to tell.

No wonder people who were inside at the time had the impression that a bomb had exploded in their immediate vicinity. Dust and dirt raised by the sudden destruction blinded them momentarily as they staggered to their feet. Many were badly bruised and cut, while others were showered with flying glass. I learned later that roof tiles were damaged at distances of more than eight or nine kilometers from the center of the explosion. Places we lived before, like Minami and Koi, and also Ushiba, Misasa, Furue, Takasu, Kan'on and Yoshijima, are about the same distance from the center of the explosion as is Aiko's.

I got to the back of the house and I could hear voices coming from the air-raid shelter. When I called hello, Kuni Tateishi, Aiko's mother-in-law, poked her head out.

"Oh my goodness! What are you doing here?"

"Is anyone hurt? I was passing by this way ..."

Then Aiko herself appeared. Her son Ryo toddled out behind her. Aiko snapped, "Stay in there!"

"It's all right now. Why don't you all come on out and go back into the house?" I said. As I walked toward the back door, they started following me.

We went inside, removed the broken glass, fragments of wall mortar and other wreckage, and then sat down in the room facing onto the little garden in back.

Then I noticed a child just about Ryo's age clinging to Aiko's mother-in-law's hand.

"Who is that?" I asked.

As soon as I asked the question, Mrs. Tateishi began telling me everything that had happened since the morning.

Her husband, Saichiro, had been called out by the voluntary services unit of the Chugoku Newspaper, where he worked, and was assigned to house demolition in the vicinity of the prefectural offices. Aiko's sister-in-law, Kimie, a student at the girls' commercial middle school, had also left to take part in a volunteer demolition project near Tsurumi Bridge that her school had organized. The older sister-in-law, Fukiyo Ueda, who was married and lived in the neighborhood, had been called out too, by the town voluntary group. She left her child with her mother and went off to work not far from that same bridge. This was the little child with Mrs. Tateishi.

All three of them had set out fairly early to be at their destinations by the appointed time of eight in the morning. Aiko had left the house a little after eight, on some errand. Aiko's brother-in-law, Hisaichi, was a member of the local defense corps and was staying at the national school in Noboricho. His sister, Kazuko, had been stationed for some time at the army hospital as chief nurse. So Mrs. Tateishi and her two grandchildren were the only ones at home.

Mrs. Tateishi had been upstairs for some time, as had the children, but once Aiko left, she had taken them downstairs so that she could open the shop. They had just walked in when the flash of yellowish light shot through the building. She crouched, throwing an arm around each of the children. Immediately she felt a strong blast of air and everything went dark. The next thing she knew, she and the children were covered with dust, thick clouds of which filled the entire house. Furniture and small items were scattered all over.

Like everyone else, she assumed a bomb had exploded somewhere close by. Mrs. Tateishi tentatively moved her arms and legs and found to her relief that she was not incapacitated, and in fact not even injured. Both grandchildren seemed to be unhurt, too. Holding them in her arms, she stood up and then picked her way through the maze of furniture and debris to the back door. From there it was a short dash into the air-raid shelter.

But just as she put the children down and heaved a sigh of relief, she heard a familiar voice calling out, loudly, outside the shelter, "Somebody, please! Is anybody in there?"

Leaving the children inside, she scrambled up to see what was going on. There, lying in the vegetable garden in front of his house, was the man who lived in the rental house in back. He was covered in blood and naked except for a loincloth. Two or three neighbors had already come running. Even his white loincloth was wet with blood. Fragments of broken glass that had pierced his skin could be seen glinting here and there all over his body. I believe the people carried him into his house and gave him first aid. It seemed the man had set out, wearing only a loincloth, to work in his vegetable garden after breakfast. Just as he stepped outside, the force of the blast had splintered the pane of glass in the door into tiny fragments.

The bloody, injured people I had seen before seemed to have been cut by glass as well. I learned later that many people had received injuries of this kind at distances of about three kilometers from the center of the explosion and, in some cases, at distances exceeding four kilometers.

Aiko, who I understand had only returned shortly before I arrived, told the following story. She had left home a little after eight in the morning and was walking along the path on the bank of the Enko River, toward Taisho Bridge. She was wearing the white short-sleeved blouse with black stripes that you made for her, a pair of *monpe* work pants and a new pair of wooden *geta* clogs. She was holding an open sun parasol in her right hand and the cloth carryall with wooden handgrips that you made for her

as a match to your own, in her left. She was walking quickly,
hoping to finish her task before another air-raid alarm could
sound. She took the Ozuguchi railroad crossing of the Ujina
Line. There are rows of houses on both sides of the road a little
further on, but where Aiko was, there are only houses on one
side. The other side of the road looks out onto the river. You
know the place.

She said it happened right at that moment. Like you, she was
suddenly exposed to an immensely powerful flash of light. At
about the same time came the tremendous roaring sound and the
blast of air. At that instant, Aiko thought a time bomb had exploded nearby. No one knew the truth about the so-called "time
bomb" but there were a lot of rumors going around about it at
the time. I thought it interesting that a young woman like Aiko
should think of a "time bomb" instead of an ordinary bomb. Hit
suddenly by deafening air pressure, Aiko felt as if she had been
spun around wildly two or three times, and was surprised to find
that she was still on her feet. She couldn't see anything for a moment and she felt slightly dizzy. When she recovered, she noticed
the parasol she had been holding in her right hand was now gone,
as was the carryall she'd had in her other hand.

Looking around, she saw the parasol, wedged half-shut, lying
under the eaves of a house to her right. She picked it up and saw
that some of its ribs were broken. Her carryall was lying on the
ground in front of her. The sole of her left foot felt strange, so she
took off her clog and found that it had split right across the middle, from left to right. Her work pants were torn straight down
the left leg. She felt some stiffness in her face but she didn't seem
to have any real injuries at all.

"Help!"

"It hurts!"

She could hear cries coming from the nearby houses. She picked
up her carryall, managed to close the parasol and hurried home.

When she got there, she didn't go in the house proper but
into the air-raid shelter, where Ryo immediately toddled up and

clung to her. It wasn't until Aiko attempted to breast-feed him that she noticed that the left side of the front of her blouse was in shreds. Only the black-striped portions seemed to be scorched.

While she spoke, Aiko had been grimacing, as if with pain. I asked her what was wrong. She said that the whole left side of her upper body, from her face down to her shoulder and breast, was gradually starting to feel burned, and that the pain was getting to be almost unbearable. I hadn't noticed until then, but I looked more closely and was startled to see that she was indeed badly burned.

I asked if there was any ointment available but was told that there wasn't. I asked about cooking oil, but there was none of that either. (As you know, cooking oil was so scarce it was practically unheard-of at the time. It's the same now though, too.) Anyway, we cleared a space in the living room by pushing aside the jumble of furniture, pulled some bedding out of a closet, and laid Aiko on it. She seemed to be in considerable pain but there was nothing else we could do. There was no doctor in the neighborhood. Even if there had been, we probably would not have been able to have him come to the house.

Mrs. Tateishi, who'd been outside, slipped in just then through the back door. "What's going to happen to us? There's a terrible fire off toward the city," she said, her voice tense.

I went outside and looked to the west. The pillar of clouds that I had seen before had been completely replaced now by massive clouds of reddish black smoke. The actual fires could not be seen, because they were blocked by Hijiyama Hill and the houses in the foreground, but it was clear that a huge fire was in progress, and it looked as if it was ravaging the entire city of Hiroshima.

At that moment, I became anxious about your and Kinji's safety and about the fate of our house.* I also began thinking about the university and my office there.

---

* [The author and his wife had three children: Kazuko (in 1945, aged 11), Keiichi (9) and Kinji (7). At the time, children between the ages of about 8 and 12 from major industrial cities were being evacuated with their classmates to the countryside. So neither of the older children was in Hiroshima.]

I went back inside, and found that Mrs. Tateishi was getting very worried about her husband and four children. No wonder. Judging from the disastrous scene outside, the fate of anyone who had gone into the city was extremely uncertain.

I was at my wits' end. There was nothing I could tell her to allay her fears and I had no idea how to treat Aiko's burns. Anxieties of my own were starting to gnaw at me too. When Aiko muttered, "I wonder if Fumiyo is all right," all three of us fell silent.

Then there came an urgent rattling at the shop door, followed by a young girl's frightened cry of "Mother!"

"My God, it's Kimie!" cried Mrs. Tateishi, rushing outside barefoot.

In a moment, we could see Kimie come into the backyard through the gate, leaning heavily on her mother. She let go and plopped onto the edge of the raised veranda, almost collapsing there. "Water, please, Mother," she pleaded.

Mrs. Tateishi picked up an aluminum cup she saw lying on the ground and went over to a faucet to get some water.

Kimie was wearing just an undershirt and a pair of *monpe* pants. The undershirt was covered with dirt and drenched with perspiration. Sweat, mixed with dirt, was streaming down her face. One of her feet was bare. Her work pants were ripped in places and hanging down in shreds. But she showed no signs of either bleeding or burns. At first, she was panting, her shoulders heaving, but she eventually became calmer and started to tell us what had happened to her.

At eight o'clock, Kimie and her classmates had assembled at the eastern foot of Tsurumi Bridge. After listening to the teacher's instructions about their work for the day, she took off her blouse and put it, together with her lunch box and canteen, down at the side of the road with the other children's. Just as they had started clearing away the remains of houses that had been demolished to create firebreaks,* Kimie was hit by a brilliant flash

---

* [The demolition of houses to create firebreaks along the main streets of the city began in April 1945 and continued at a rapid pace throughout the subsequent months.]

of light. At nearly the same moment, she felt as if she'd been hit by a fierce blast of air. She passed out.

When she came to, she had no idea how much time had gone by. She could see nothing but the yellow dust that filled the air. Then she realized she was trapped under some old beams and pieces of lumber. She tried moving her arms and legs and found that she could, and that she felt no pain anywhere. She could see a few of her schoolmates, trapped too. She heard girls crying, calling for their mothers.

Kimie struggled free from the pile of debris and stood up. Still there was no pain. People were running across the bridge. She noticed that scattered piles of rubble were starting to burn, giving off smoke. She started to run as fast as she could, thinking that if she stayed around any longer she would burn to death. Soon she got to the road and started running northward. Some people were running the other way. There were boys and girls about her age and many adults. Some people had blood streaming from their heads; other people's clothes were stained with blood. One man's arm was dangling in a peculiar way and he was holding onto it with his other hand; some people were limping along, obviously in great pain. Flames and smoke were rising everywhere.

When Kimie reached the front of Hijiyama Shrine, she saw the houses ahead burning furiously. So she turned off the road and ran up the hill, along the side of the shrine. A lot of other people were climbing the hill too. When she got to the open space at the top, where the old Gobenden building was, a crowd was already gathered there. Looking down, she could see the entire city of Hiroshima on fire. She looked to the east, toward her home, and felt a little relieved when she could see neither smoke nor fire. So she decided to return home. She scrambled down the hill toward the back of the school, which had collapsed but was not burning. No one whom she asked knew what had become of any of the teachers or the other students.

That was where Kimie left off her story. She had been hit by the blast of the explosion and still had escaped almost completely

unscathed. Later, I heard stories from others of similarly miracu-
lous escapes. It's strange how the difference between life and
death can be decided by simple quirks of fate in cases like these.

As Kimie spoke, I became more and more worried about our
house, the university and our department. Besides, the house of
Mototsugu Kurita, who was head of our department, was near
the center of the city. So after I had tried to console Mrs. Tateishi
and offered a few words of encouragement to Aiko, I left their
house. I set off in the direction of Higashi-ohashi Bridge, deciding to go first to the top of Hijiyama Hill to get a general view of
the city before deciding on my next course of action.

I never had opportunity to revisit them after that. It was some
time after your funeral when Aiko, who had recovered from her
burns by then, visited me, that I first had any further news. Aiko
had likewise heard nothing about us and was shocked and grieved
to learn of your passing. However, tragedies of this sort were
quite common in Hiroshima at the time. Everyone suffered, more
or less. It was rare for a family not to have one or two members
dead, missing or injured. Often people had no news of, and no
way to get in touch with, members of their own family living in
the same city.

It turned out that Aiko's husband's family suffered a great deal.
Although Aiko's sister-in-law, Fukiyo, came home that evening
badly burned, she made good progress from then on and eventually recovered fully. But Aiko's father-in-law, Saichiro, who had
been helping with house demolition, could not be found even
after numerous searches. The only things of his that were ever
found were his watch chain and his lunch box, left together in the
workers' rest area. Their daughter, Kazuko, who as I mentioned
was chief nurse at the army hospital, was killed when the hospital
collapsed. Her ashes were returned to the family a few days later.
Aiko's young brother-in-law, Hisaichi, was badly injured at the
national school in Noboricho when he was trapped under the
rubble of the building. He managed to crawl out before any fires
started, and was sent to the army hospital in Hesaka. He went

back home after being treated for a few days, but he died after about a week of great pain.

So Aiko has had a rough time of it. Worst of all, she has no idea what happened to her husband, Ryotaro, who was in the army.

—November 20, 1945

Fumiyo Yoshizaki in her twenties, before her marriage.

A City Transformed

August 6, 1945

Fumiyo,

It was about noon when I got to the top of Hijiyama Hill. After leaving Aiko's, I was in such a hurry that I hardly noticed anything about the condition of the people I passed or the roads I walked along. When I came out alongside the girl's commercial middle school, I ran toward the top of the hill and the pavilion there. When I reached the top, I looked down over the city and was transfixed.

I imagine that the sight of Hiroshima so horribly transformed will stay with me for the rest of my life. Little more than three hours had elapsed since the blinding flash, and in those hours Hiroshima had ceased to exist. Japan's seventh largest city, with a population of four hundred thousand, had disappeared. Known as a "water metropolis" because it was built on the white deltas formed by the clear waters of seven rivers, the city was now burned and dry. It turned out that those three hours were really no different than an instant. I learned later that the city's transformation did take place instantaneously, at the moment of the bluish flash of light.

I couldn't believe it. All around me was a vast sea of smoking rubble and debris, with a few concrete buildings rising here and there like pale tombstones, many of them shrouded in smoke. That's all there was, as far as the eye could see.

The hills of Koi, normally visible far in the distance to the west, now appeared very close. The flat land leading up to those hills was a mass of blackened, smoldering rubble, dotted with the ghostlike remains of concrete buildings. That's all there was.

Through breaks in the clouds of smoke, the island of Miyajima could be seen in the distance, unchanged, in the sea far off to the left, but the area near Mount Futaba, close by on the right, was on fire.

With the features of the city so completely changed, I couldn't determine which direction was which. I looked a long time for the main building of our university. I finally found it: a big, brown three-storey building, quite close by below on the left, amid fire and smoke. To its right was the smart grey elementary school affiliated with the university, the school our own children attended. There were no buildings where the teachers' college and its affiliated middle school should have been. They had all been completely destroyed.

Beyond the university buildings, I could see the hills of Eba. A group of cranes was clearly visible in the shipyards built on the reclaimed land to the left of the hills. No fire or smoke was evident in the vicinity of the Eba hills or the adjoining industrial area. Eba had not burned to the ground!

Just then my thoughts turned to our house in Funairi and I became worried about you and Kinji. I looked over toward the right. A considerable area extending down from the Eba hills was not burned. Funairi-kawaguchicho, where our house was, seemed to be safe for the time being, but the area around Funairi-honcho looked as if it had burned. I began to feel uneasy again, realizing that even if our house was still standing, that wouldn't necessarily mean that you were safe.

I'd been so engrossed in looking over the city that I hadn't noticed groups of people gathering in the flat open space at the top of Hijiyama Hill where I was. Almost none had any possessions with them. Nearly everyone was barefoot; it almost looked as if they had agreed beforehand not to wear anything on their feet. It was clear that they had only just managed to escape from their homes and had fled up here in whatever they happened to be wearing at the time.

Actually, there were some women in *monpe* work pants and light, rubber-soled footwear and a number of men wearing shoes with gaiters, but these people had obviously been helping demolish houses to create firebreaks. Some people wore makeshift bandages, made from towels, handkerchiefs or torn-up shirts.

Almost everyone was either sitting on the ground, eyes cast downward, or standing around gazing vacantly over the devastation. They were not so much looking at the scene before them as passively letting it sink in. They appeared oblivious to the heat of the midsummer sun. It was as if they had lost all feeling and grown indifferent to the world around them.

A few people weaved aimlessly through the crowds, looking for families and loved ones. "Is so-and-so from such-and-such a place here?" someone would shout once in a while.

Children called out for parents with shrill, tearful cries. Some children just wandered along by themselves, wailing. Others—in many cases, very small children—stood quietly off to the side.

People were talking in hushed, subdued tones. Fear welled up in me again and I tried to imagine how Hiroshima could have been totally destroyed. Were hundreds of bombs and thousands of incendiaries dropped together? But I knew that that wasn't it, because there were no large formations of planes overhead at the time. There was no answer except that it must be some kind of new weapon.

Just then, I saw a man who looked like an army officer surveying the crowd. I walked up to him and asked, "What's happened?"

"What?" he said, giving me a rather hostile look.

I then realized that I must look out of place among the bedraggled people gathered there. And I was apparently not a member of any defense corps or rescue party. There was no one there who looked less like a local inhabitant than I did at that moment. Perhaps he took me for a spy.

Then I remembered the calling cards listing my name and profession that I carried around but hated using. I fumbled around in my pocket, found one and handed it to him.

He seemed to relax a little. Then he said in a somewhat abashed tone, "Actually, I graduated from the university's science department." That made sense; he did suddenly look like a student to me.

"Frankly, I think it was an atomic bomb," he said in a low voice.

I doubted my own ears.

"An atomic bomb!"

"Yes."

"What? The one made with uranium ...?"

"Yes. Apart from the theoretical problems, I have heard that it's not even technologically feasible to produce that kind of bomb in Japan yet. But considering that a single explosion has caused this much destruction, I think it must have been an atomic bomb, although I admit I don't really know much about it," he replied.

He was being modest, but his tone was thoughtful and confident. I wanted to ask him all kinds of questions but I could see that he was already preoccupied with the crowd again.

"Well, thanks very much," I said,

"Excuse me, sir. I've got to hurry." He saluted and ran off down the hill.

I hastily tried to recall any information I had read or heard on the atomic bomb. My knowledge was spotty at best, but there were no great inconsistencies between what I did know and the things I myself had experienced that morning.

"A matchbox full of uranium would be enough to blow up Mt. Fuji," I remembered someone telling me. That must be what it was, I thought. It must have been an atomic bomb.

I looked down again at the fires and blackened ruins in the city and then turned my gaze back to the refugees around me. I recalled the bombings and incendiary attacks I had experienced in the past. This was different, totally different. A single explosion had produced more devastation than ten or twenty large air raids.

I remembered a roundtable discussion I had read in a science magazine—maybe *Asahi Science*—in which leaders in various fields talked about the atomic bomb. I especially remember that one literary scholar had remarked, "Once that bomb is perfected, there will be no more war." Strangely, those words suddenly made me feel hopeful. This will bring an end to the war, I thought.

Yet my next thought was completely cynical. As you know, I was scheduled to go, the next day, east to the factory of Nippon Steel Manufacturing Company as supervising instructor of a students' labor squad.* Yet I was suddenly certain that Japan had lost the war.

I spat on the ground hard, without thinking. Despite the overwhelming evidence before my eyes that the war was over, I still had to go to the factory the next day to help make hand grenades. I was scheduled to assist in the production of that most primitive of "scientific" weapons, the hand grenade, after just having witnessed the work of an extraordinarily powerful weapon. But I was in no position to disobey the order. I knew from past experience what it would be like at the factory. The government had recently decided to ignore the Potsdam Declaration of July 26. Everyone was sure the government would advocate fighting a "decisive battle" on the Japanese mainland, amid promises of an "honorable death for a hundred million people." As an instructor supervising student workers at the factory, I was expected to pass on such sentiments to the students working there.

I feel a bit ridiculous when I look back on it now and think about my lack of understanding of the real situation. In the initial stages of the conflict, I did have a certain amount of faith in the war Japan was fighting, and had intended to do my part. But after

---

* [Beginning in 1941, the government began a systematic program of inducing people to work in weapons manufacturing. By 1944 nearly 1.8 million older students were at work and formal school lessons were reduced to one or two hours per day (provided that the schools were still standing).]

the communiqués regarding the "strategic retreat" of Japanese forces from Guadalcanal were issued, I began to have my doubts. You, at least, must have been aware of this. But I was unable to transform these doubts into convictions and so simply continued to deceive myself. Not only that, I forced others to accept this deception as well.

That's the way I was living my life. That's how I was supporting you and the children. I had fully resigned myself to my own cowardice. And yet at the same time I had begun to despise myself. I hardly ever spoke about these feelings with you when you were alive. Now, standing at the top of this hill, I realized my self-deception was finally starting to fall away. I had no idea what I should do now.

You always simply—or should I say naively and honestly—cooperated in the war effort without uttering a word of complaint. You would only say, "Until we win the war ..." But you must have been exhausted by the sleepless nights as the air raids got worse toward the end of the war, by the frequent calls for so-called "voluntary service" which could not be ignored for the very real fear of looking "unpatriotic" to your acquaintances, by the daily scrounging for food amid diminishing supplies and by other hardships of war. You, too, would have been vastly relieved to know that the war was coming to an end. Everyone in Japan must have felt that way.

But to go back to my story, I was about to descend the hill when I unexpectedly ran into Mrs. Sugimoto, the wife of my colleague, Naojiro Sugimoto. I think you've met her. She was wearing what appeared to be her everyday clothes, *monpe* work pants and *geta* clogs. The clogs caught my attention because very few people on the hill had anything on their feet. She appeared to be free of any injury or burns. Soon Professor Sugimoto came up behind her. You must remember him; he visited our house several times.

"Hello. What are you doing up here?" he said.

"I just happened to be nearby."

"How's your house?"

"I don't know. How's yours?"

"It burned down. We were down below at first but there are so many injured people there we decided to come up here. We're homeless."

"That's too bad."

We moved off the roadside, away from the others, and sat down under a pine tree, where the Sugimotos told me what had happened to them.

Thinking about it now, it seems like I must have been in a strangely relaxed state of mind to dawdle like that. But maybe that's what people are inclined to do under these kind of circumstances.

The Sugimotos' home was at the foot of Hijiyama Hill, a bit off to the west. After breakfast, Mrs. Sugimoto had gone out to work in the vegetable garden in the backyard, but had returned to the kitchen to get something. Since he was preparing to go out, Mr. Sugimoto had changed into his suit and then, instead of going upstairs to his study, had sat down to read a book at a low table on the tatami mat floor. Just then, there was a brilliant flash, followed by a thunderous roar. Mr. Sugimoto said that his first thought was that the house had been hit directly by a bomb. For a while, he couldn't see anything at all, although he remained fully conscious. He was able to move his hands, but then found that his upper body was restrained somehow. As his eyesight gradually came back, he realized he was pinned down where he was, leaning over the table, by a heavy pile of boards and plaster. He realized too that he'd been blinded temporarily by the dust raised by the sudden upheaval. Strangely, he'd never felt that his life was in any danger. He'd simply mused that the enemy needn't have deliberately dropped a bomb on a house such as theirs, or that a stray shell from the antiaircraft battery on top of the hill must have fallen onto the house.

After wriggling his arms and legs free, he was able to struggle to his feet. He looked around and saw that the free-standing screen which had stood at the front entrance, as well as the kitchen table and the partition walls, had all been swept over to one side of the house, and that boards from the ceiling and walls had collapsed together in a heap. He himself had been ensconced in a tiny cavity created by the table, which had served to prop up some of the fallen lumber and boards. He realized he'd had a narrow escape. He called out to his wife. She was safe too, caught between some lumber and walls that had been dislodged but that hadn't completely given way.

He then suddenly remembered that he was supposed to take charge of a group of students assigned to the army marine corps at Ujina, a port city south of Hiroshima. He made his way to the front door and looked for his shoes, but couldn't find them. The hard earthen floor of the entryway was riddled with glass, tiles and lumber. He heard his wife call out, "The laundry balcony upstairs is on fire!"

"I can't do anything about it right now. I've got to get to Ujina!" he shouted, dashing out. He was wearing a suit, but was without shoes or a hat. Looking at his house from the outside, he saw that the second floor was strangely twisted and compressed onto the first, giving the whole house a squashed appearance. All the houses in the neighborhood looked similar, with some being completely flattened. He heard cries and screams coming from various houses but he kept on running, with only one thought in mind: getting to Ujina. Broken glass and roof tiles were scattered over the road, and he worried about his feet. Fortunately, he didn't hurt himself.

He came to the street where the streetcars usually run and saw that it was packed with people looking for refuge. Some were running north to south, others in the opposite direction. Houses on either side of the street had collapsed, and tongues of flame flickered here and there in the wreckage. The smoke reminded him of his wife's cries about the burning laundry balcony. For a minute, he considered retracing his steps but thought, no, he must get to Ujina, and kept running.

On the way, several people asked him for directions to rescue stations. He knew nothing at all about such matters. But on seeing how badly injured they were, he would point toward Hijiyama Hill and tell them, on the spur of the moment, "Go there." This quick-witted advice may have been instrumental in saving a lot of lives since as it turned out a rescue station had indeed been established there. People's injuries were terrible: some were coated in blood; some had on clothes that were burned to tatters, beneath which the skin was discolored and swollen. Some people's clothes were still smoldering; he helped put them out. One little girl was wearing only panties, her skin completely blackened, with bits of burned clothing stuck to it; a middle-aged woman who'd lost all her clothes had wrapped something that looked like a straw mat around her lower body. All of these people were shuffling along, without energy or strength to go any faster. Figures could be seen scattered at intervals on the roadside—probably those who were badly injured or already dead.

When he approached Hijiyama Bridge, he saw that the area between Takeyacho and the university was burning furiously. The bridge was packed with people fleeing. Many people were also running eastward along the foot of the hill, or toward Minamicho and Ujina in the south. "There's a rescue station at the army clothing depot," somebody said.

Looking back, he could see thick smoke rising from the area around Hijiyama Hill, smoke that was as dense as it was in the center of the city. Our house must have burned down, he thought as he ran along the track, avoiding the occasional streetcar that was stopped along it.

He was covered in sweat and dirt when he got to Ujina. Many injured civilians were gathered there, in the grounds of the army transport section. Some of the buildings in the compound had been destroyed, but most were intact. Some students from his university were there but none was seriously injured. Mr. Sugimoto was given a pair of rubber-soled footwear, which freed him from worries about injuring his bare feet. He boarded an army ship that was headed for Kanawa Island.

As you may know, the army marine corps at Ujina was called the "Akatsuki Butai" (dawn corps). Its work was performed at three different locations: the transportation section in Ujina, the shipbuilding yard on Kanawa Island and the Taibi warehouse at Sakamura, across the island. The main tasks of the personnel in this corps were building small vessels and transporting military supplies to the front.

When he reached Kanawa Island, Mr. Sugimoto found that there was even less damage there than in Ujina. After confirming that his students on the island were safe, he retraced his steps and started back to the university, where he planned to make his report. When he got there though, he found that it had burned almost to the ground, and that the only people there were Kanae Watanabe, chief of air-raid precautions at the university, and a few clerical personnel.

He managed to travel back to his house, though he had to fight his way through fire and smoke a number of times. The house was now little more than ashes. The study had fallen straight down to the ground floor and piles of books were lying there burning gaily. He didn't know where his wife had gone but he'd come up to the top of Hijiyama Hill and eventually found her there, safe and sound.

The even tone and the calm with which Mr. Sugimoto related all these experiences to me were characteristic of his lecture style, but made him seem a bit oblivious to the extraordinary events taking place around him.

After he'd left the house to go to Ujina, he said, his wife had dashed out through the back door. By then the fire on the laundry balcony had spread to the house. She had locked the door of the air-raid shelter, where she had laid in some emergency supplies, and had rushed off to the safety of Hijiyama Hill.

Then Mrs. Sugimoto finally spoke for the first time, and it was to mutter, "We might have been able to save some of our belongings if my husband had stayed home." This remark pricked at my conscience. I became worried all over again about our house and about you and Kinji.

I looked at my watch; it was past three. Seven hours had elapsed since the flash. Mr. Sugimoto said that he and his wife would go and get futons and mosquito nets from their air-raid shelter and would spend the night there on the hill. So I left them and proceeded down the hill. I had to get home and see how things were there.

—November 25, 1945

Kazuko Ogura (at extreme left) at the temple in the mountains where she and her classmates were living, spring 1945.

The Inferno

August 6, 1945

Fumiyo,

On my way down Hijiyama Hill, after I'd parted with Professor Sugimoto and his wife, I ran into your brother Hideichi's wife, Kiyoko.

She had the two younger children with her, one clutching at each of her hands. Each child was also holding a rice ball, which had probably been given to them at a rescue station. Your sister-in-law was drenched with sweat and her wet summer housedress, blackened with cinders and dust, clung to her.

"What happened?" I asked as I approached her. She didn't answer at first; she looked utterly exhausted. I helped her and the children over to a shady spot on the grass under a tree and had them sit down. Soon she began to tell me.

At the time of the bombing, your brother was not at home; he had left for work already. Kiyoko was washing some clothes in the kitchen. Their daughter, Eiko, who was too frail to go off with her classmates to live in the countryside where it was safer, was cleaning the living room. The two smaller children were playing in front of the house.

Just then, there was a flash of light and the house groaned and shuddered, and began to collapse. Kiyoko made a wild dash for the outside and, hugging the two young children in her arms, crouched down, stunned.

"Mother!" Eiko's screams soon brought her back to her senses. By then, the house had completely collapsed before her eyes, amid thick clouds of dust. The screams were coming from underneath the crushed house. She immediately pushed the other children away and rushed to the spot where she heard the screams.

"Mother! It hurts!"

Eiko's agonized cries continued. Her mother frenziedly threw aside roof tiles, pulled away boards and dragged heavy lumber from the spot, shouting loudly as she did so, "Someone please come help me!"

But no one came. Of course, looking back on it now, you can't blame people. Everyone in the neighborhood was in a similar situation.

Kiyoko kept shouting for help as she continued her efforts but, regrettably, there is a limit to what one woman can do on her own, and there wasn't even a saw or any other tool handy. She felt utterly frustrated and powerless. Suddenly she heard someone yell, "Fire!" Looking around, she saw that all the houses in the neighborhood had been flattened by the blast and that smoke was rising here and there from the debris. Small fires could also be seen. Startled, she looked back at the other two children and saw them cowering. There were no fires close to the ruins of her house yet. Looking out onto the street, she could see crowds of people heading for Hijiyama Hill. She ordered the children to flee to Hijiyama. But they were terrified and refused. She took their hands and dragged them onto the street. "Follow these people and go with them to Hijiyama. I'll join you there later," she said, shoving them into the moving stream of people.

Returning to the ruins of her house, she saw smoke start to rise from the area that had been the backyard. Tongues of flame flickered up, then disappeared. There's no hope now, she thought, but she continued trying to remove the debris imprisoning her daughter. The girl's intermittent pleas grew weaker, and her cries of "It hurts!" changed to "It's hot!" The heat of the flames had obviously started to seep beneath the pile of debris. Soon Kiyoko herself was being showered with flying sparks, and the flames around the area were growing higher. The smoke was so thick now she couldn't see a thing. The house itself started to burn with a loud crackling sound. Soon she couldn't stand the shower of hot sparks or the heat from the fires all around any longer. There was nothing else that she could do.

"Forgive me, Eiko," her heart cried out. She fled, running.

"Mother, it's hot!" Eiko's voice seemed to follow her no matter how far she ran. It was unbearable. She ran blindly, repeating over and over in her heart, "Forgive me, Eiko." On her way to the hill, she heard cries for help several times. Each time, she felt it was her daughter calling. Once she turned toward the sound of a cry with a shudder of anticipation and saw someone wedged under a collapsed roof, the upper half of his or her body protruding, arms clawing at the ground. Another time, she saw just a head and one arm sticking out from a pile of rubble. But no one stopped to help anyone. So it wasn't only with Eiko. She felt a slight sense of resignation.

She finally got to Hijiyama Hill and started looking for the other two. She found them after a long search but couldn't get Eiko out of her mind. She told the two children, who were crying by then, to stay where they were and went back down the hill. The house was completely burned down now and the heat was so strong it was impossible to even go down the alleyway leading to it.

"I just got back here a while ago," she said to me, grimly. I couldn't look her in the face.

"Umm ..." was all I could murmur.

As your sister-in-law spoke, I became so worried about you and Kinji that I was almost beside myself. I told her that since her husband's company, Toyo Kogyo, was five or six hundred meters east of Shin'ozu Bridge, where I had seen the flash, he must be all right, and that he would, no doubt, come looking for them soon. To make her feel better, I also said I'd put up a placard at the corner of the alleyway near their house, saying that she was on the hilltop with the two children. The children had been silent the whole time, as if they were in a trance. They showed no interest in eating the rice balls in their hands.

I heard that several days later your brother, Hideichi, recovered Eiko's bones from the ruins of their house. They were found clean and bleached white, under a big, burned-out wooden beam.

I know how shocked and saddened you would have been to know about poor Eiko's fate.

Tragic stories like this were not uncommon at the time. The wife and child of your brother, Tetsuji Tanaka, who lived across the road from us, were rescued from beneath the ruins of their house, whereas a middle-aged woman who lived nearby and happened to be visiting Tetsuji's at the time was found a few days later under some burned debris; again, there was nothing left but bones. You remember that student of mine—a few years older than the others—who visited us two or three times this spring? He lost his wife and child. He'd taken a few days off from his factory work to make preparations for evacuating his family to the provinces, and was back with them in the house they rented in Kakocho. He was just coming out of the bathroom when it happened. By some miracle, he escaped without a scratch. His wife and child, though, were trapped under a big wooden beam. He tried desperately to get them out but the lower half of his wife's body was pinned, and he could not free her. The baby in her arms had apparently been killed instantly, but she'd remained conscious. As he was trying frantically to get her out, the fire had grown stronger and begun to rage fiercely all around him. In the end, he'd had to flee to save his own life. Since that tragedy, he visits me frequently—to seek the compassion of someone else who was there, I suppose. He came just the other day and we talked for a while. He told me more than once that he'd never be able to forget his wife's voice when she pleaded with him to leave her there and save himself—or her face, when he finally did.

I don't know whether he says it out of envy or to console me when he says, "Professor, you're one of the luckier ones."

Mr. Otsuka, governor of the Chugoku district,* whose provisional offices had been set up on the third floor of our university, met with disaster at his official residence near Nagaregawa. The flash occurred just as he was leaving for his office and he became trapped under the ruins of his home. His family and his assistants were struggling in the midst of a raging fire to release him when he gave strict orders for them to stop and run to safety. The newspaper accounts said that he met death bravely and calmly. If such stoic behavior is considered ideal under the circumstances, then there was no lack of similarly inspiring stories to be found in the city at that time.

After leaving Kiyoko, I practically ran down the gently sloping roadway on Hijiyama Hill. I was now very worried about you and Kinji, and went as quickly as I could.

But a minute later I saw something that brought me to an abrupt halt. A swarm of people, all of them burned or injured, was teeming up the long, wide roadway. They looked like fragments or scraps of living organisms, motivated not by any personal desire to seek refuge but by some vast, tenacious "life force" that transcended individual will. I can't describe the scene adequately, but that was my impression when I caught sight of them coming up the roadway.

The midsummer sun was beating down fiercely. I had not noticed this before, but the leaves of all the trees growing on that slope were scorched brown. People were squatting or lying on the road under these trees and on the slopes of the hill above and below the roadway—people with injuries and burns, people who were partly or completely naked. Their injuries and burns were even worse than those Kimie and Professor Sugimoto had described a short while earlier. People's skin was discolored and swollen. I'd seen the burns that Aiko suffered, but these were nothing like that. These were deep pink, or rather like the color of rotten loquats or peeled tomatoes. The skin of some people

---

* [The Chugoku district spans the entire western part of Honshu, comprising Hiroshima, Okayama, Shimane, Tottori and Yamaguchi prefectures.]

appeared to be glistening in the sun but, when I looked closer, I would see that the skin had peeled off like that of a ripe peach and was hanging down loosely. I saw one person whose entire facial skin had peeled off, from the hairline down, and was hanging from their cheeks and chin. Another person's skin had been flayed off both arms and was drooping down from the wrists. People with skin peeled cleanly off their backs reminded me of carcasses you see hanging in butcher shops. There were objects that appeared to be lumps of flesh lying on the ground. Some of these squirmed from time to time, like exhibits in a freak show at a fair ground. The people with run-of-the-mill injuries could still easily be recognized as human and so seemed to be playing supporting roles in this horrible drama.

I saw much more than I could bear. I stood rooted to the spot at first, but was soon overwhelmed and ran the rest of the way down.

When I reached the bottom of the hill, quite a few trucks were parked in the road where the streetcars normally ran. Some military personnel and men who looked like security guards were shouting out orders. Civilians who seemed unhurt or only slightly wounded were piling onto the trucks. When a truck was loaded to overflowing, it would move off. Some headed in the direction of Ujina, and others toward Hiroshima Station. I never saw them turn down anyone who wanted to board.

The stark spectacle was far beyond anything I had imagined from the top of the hill. From that vantage, the land had looked very bare, but I had assumed that I simply couldn't see anything because of the distance. Once down here though, I could see that there truly was nothing left. All the houses had been leveled and burned, their remains forming mounds in a field of burning, smoking debris. Large whitish concrete structures were visible in the distance. That's all there was. It was exactly the same as the view from the top of the hill. There was no difference at all between the distant view and the scene close-up. That was what astounded me.

This particular street hadn't been visible from the hilltop. Stretching from north to south and newly equipped with lines for streetcar service, it was bounded now on either side by expanses of black ruins. Apart from a few people and trucks, nothing was moving on the street. Streetcars stood motionless. Electric power lines and telephone poles lay where they had fallen. Steel supports used to suspend power cables over the streetcar lines were twisted and broken at their foundations. All the poles and structures lay pointing in the same direction—east. It was eerily quiet. Dead bodies dotted the street in a chain of black lumps.

I felt as if I had climbed down to the bottom of a volcanic crater. Fires were still smoldering, and this was only one small corner of the inferno. Visions of classic scroll paintings I had seen that depicted Buddhist versions of hell sprang to mind. I shuddered at the thought of the scenes that might greet me as I walked toward the actual site of the flash. I thought that what I had seen before might have prepared me. But most of what I knew was gleaned from the accounts given by Aiko, Kimie, Professor Sugimoto and your sister-in-law Kiyoko, all of whom happened to be two to three kilometers away from the center of the explosion. I realized later that the degree of devastation increased exponentially as one approached the site of the explosion.

I started walking alongside the streetcar lines, where there was less obstruction. The only obstacles there were the fallen utility poles and severed electrical wires scattered over the ground. Burned-out streetcars stood motionless in their tracks, the scorched steel plates on their sides glinting red in the sun. I encountered any number of dead but they didn't slow my progress. I averted my eyes whenever I passed a corpse. Smoke and small residual flames were rising everywhere from the debris. The heat from the remains was greater than that of the sun overhead. It was like walking around in a big furnace that had been shut off just a moment before.

As I walked, I noticed that there was no evidence of shrapnel or bomb craters. Nor did I see any traces of spent incendiaries or live bombs. If the destruction had been caused by an atomic bomb, this was to be expected. And I was becoming fairly sure, by this time, that an atomic bomb was involved. Nevertheless, past experience made me keep an eye out. I did think it strange that I had not seen a single earthen warehouse. I'd seen some caved-in roofs and collapsed white walls that could have been the remnants of such warehouses, but only rarely. The force of the explosion seemed to have caused many of these to vanish without a trace. The landscape here was entirely different from that of a city that had been the target of incendiary bombing.

I was becoming concerned whether I would ever find the spot where your brother Hideichi's house had stood. As you know, we always used the Danbara national school as our landmark for finding their house. Now that school was nowhere to be seen; it had disappeared altogether. But then, by some stroke of luck, I just happened to see Hideichi standing on the roadside with his bicycle, gazing vacantly around.

"Hello! Isn't it terrible," I called out.

"Umm ..." he murmured, turning his face my way. He didn't say anything else.

I then simply told him that his family was gathered near the suspension bridge on Hijiyama Hill.

He perked up immediately. "Is that so! Then I must ..." he said, hurriedly getting onto his bicycle and cycling off.

I hadn't been able to tell him about Eiko.

While I was trying to convince myself that I had done the right thing, I arrived at the western end of the streetcar bridge at Matoba. I could see palls of black smoke and cinders rising from fires near Hiroshima Station. Looking carefully, I could even make out the main station building enveloped in smoke. Normally you wouldn't be able to see the station from where I was—now everything in between had burned to the ground.

I turned left and walked along the streetcar line that runs to Kamiyacho. The number of bodies on the road increased. Some of the people lying there still seemed to be alive. Occasionally I'd think I had seen one of them move. I sometimes thought I heard people calling out to me. But I walked on, telling myself that it was all my imagination. Without planning to, I'd adopted the motto of the three wise monkeys: see no evil, hear no evil, speak no evil. It seemed that this was the only way I could keep from losing my mind.

No matter how far I walked, the sea of ruins stretching back on both sides of the road still burned and smoked. Once in a while, flames would flare up, sending black smoke swirling and sparks flying, and some structure would collapse in a fiery heap. This triggered visions of countless victims like Eiko being burned alive while screaming for help, trapped beneath the embers, teeth tightly clenched and limbs flailing. At times, your face would appear among the victims; other times, Kinji's.

Soon I started imagining the smoldering embers rising in unison and engulfing me in flames and smoke, while I writhed in agony. I started walking faster.

I eventually came to the streetcar stop at Inaricho, on the bank of the Kyobashi River. As you know, a streetcar bridge crosses the river near there, similar to the one over the Enko River. Kyobashi Bridge, which is a little ways upstream from the streetcar bridge, was intact and a lot of people and trucks were using it. I realized later that the reason I had seen so few people between Matoba and that point was probably because there is no pedestrian bridge there and it is a fair distance from the main road. It was like that even in normal times.

The utility poles on one part of the streetcar bridge were bent and almost toppling over. The power lines were severed and hanging loose. The bridge itself seemed to be twisted and smoke was rising from its smoldering wooden rail sleepers. I saw people approaching from the other end. Heartened a bit, I started crossing the bridge, stepping from sleeper to sleeper. The river seemed to be approaching full tide, with the water flowing upstream. Dead bodies could be seen floating in the water, both upstream and downstream of the bridge. A few were jammed up against the pier just below me. I felt a strange sensation in the soles of my feet—as if I had stepped on the bodies.

Near the end of the bridge, I came across three dead bodies lying haphazardly, face up. They were all adults, and one was definitely a woman. Clumps of crinkled, burned hair lay scattered around the feet of the man's corpse next to her. The three bodies were almost naked and, to my dismay, positioned such that I would be forced to step over one of them. I thought of the man whom I'd just passed on the bridge, walking the other way. I'd seen him approaching from a distance and had noticed him step casually over something at about this spot. I could not bring myself to do that.

Since the dead woman's knees were raised slightly, I grasped the ankles to move the legs aside slightly so that I could pass without having to step over the body. But as I tried to lift the legs, I thought I felt my hands slip. It was an indescribably weird sensation. Looking down at my hands, I saw the exposed muscles of both legs, from the knees down, glinting in the sun. The color was similar to that which I'd seen on other burned people on Hijiyama Hill a short while before. The skin had peeled off and had gathered at the ankles, all wrinkled up.

I crouched there for a minute, with the shock of it. But the legs did now lie a bit to one side, and a space had opened between the body of the woman and those of the others, which I walked through. My legs were unsteady for some time afterward.

From then on, I kept my eyes down while I walked, because of the rising number of bodies on the road and the broken power lines that lay tangled everywhere like giant cobwebs. But the trouble was that when I looked down like that, I couldn't help but see the dead bodies, their faces contorted into expressions of unspeakable anguish. The countenances only got worse as I walked on. One person's eyes had popped out; the intestines of another had spilled from a burst abdomen. Humans weren't the only victims. There was a dead horse with its entrails exposed and a smashed, burned cart on top of it. Charred hulls of trucks, cars, sidecars, bicycle trailers and handcarts cluttered the roadway.

I came upon the remains of a streetcar that was burned in a way I had not seen before. It was completely destroyed. The corpse of one passenger lay on the steps. I peeked inside and saw that the floor had burned through and that dead bodies were piled up inside. Later I heard that in some streetcars passengers had been found seated side by side. On close inspection, they were all found to have burned to death instantly in whatever posture they'd happened to have assumed at that critical moment: sitting, standing with one foot on the step and so on. Having seen this streetcar, I had no trouble later believing that story.

I found myself in front of the Chugoku Newspaper building. It was a tall, slender building and I was able to recognize it immediately, even though it was badly damaged by fire. Next to it was the squat old Fukuya department store, with its tall new addition. Several gaudily painted movie theaters had stood between the new and old stores; they were reduced to ashes. Despite the theaters' solid-looking westernized exteriors, they were in fact flimsy wooden imitations. You remember, I always used to say sarcastically that this kind of structure, of which there were so many examples in Hiroshima, was typical of "new Japanese culture." Now they were obliterated, together with the wooden buildings that were representative of older, traditional Japanese culture. The only buildings that retained at least their basic shape, even if they were burned out inside, were modern, western-style ferroconcrete buildings.

I retraced my steps a little way and went back to the radio station on Kami-nagaregawa Street.

This had also been gutted, with only the skeleton of the main building still standing. I had intended to walk to Professor Kurita's house through the alleyway along the side of the building, but the whole area was still so hot from the fire that I couldn't even approach it. Trees had been plentiful in people's yards in that part of town, and their embers were still smoking. I went back to the streetcar line and started walking from in front of the Fukuya department store in Hatchobori toward the Kamiyacho crossing.

I saw quite a few people moving about in the area but most of them seemed to be engaged in rescue work. I saw almost no one who themselves seemed to be seeking refuge. It looked as if everyone who could flee had done so already. The people lying everywhere on the roads were by this point probably without exception the dead and the mortally wounded.

As I continued walking, I grew firmer in my resolve to "see no evil, hear no evil, speak no evil," and avoided talking or listening to anyone I met. Because of my experience moving the woman's corpse at the end of the streetcar bridge downstream from Kyobashi Bridge, I added a fourth prohibition: no touching.

But I broke this last rule, much to my regret. I can't remember the exact spot but I saw a burned steel helmet lying in the ashes on the roadside. In a fit of irritation, I strode up to it and kicked it hard. It rolled over, revealing a white skull inside. I stood rooted to the spot and then jumped back, aghast. The skull might well have belonged to an on-duty air-raid warden, looking manly in his uniform and helmet, when he was suddenly trapped under the debris of a house and then incinerated.

I don't know why I'd kicked that helmet. But I do know that the endless scenes of devastation had stirred up an indescribable rage in me. Who had started this pointless war? And wasn't it those same people who made the foolish gesture of ignoring the Potsdam Declaration? Didn't they realize that in a war they could *expect* people to use poison gas, V-1 and V-2 rockets and even atomic bombs? I guess I was pondering these questions when I'd seen the steel helmet sitting mutely in the ashes.

I'd reached the Kamiyacho crossing, and was so startled that I paused again. Until then, large banks and office buildings had lined the east side of the street where the streetcars ran north and south toward Takanohashi. There was the Geibi building, the Sumitomo Company, Fukoku Life Insurance, the Seiyoken Restaurant, the Hiroshima branch of the Bank of Japan, the Asano Library, the Chugoku Electric Power Company and Hiroshima City Hall, I can't remember quite all of them.

But now the entire area of the Kawayamachi Street intersection lined with those modern city buildings could be seen from where I stood at the Kamiyacho crossing, all the buildings in between having burned to the ground. These buildings had been gutted, but their outer structures stood intact, tall as ever, in neat rows. Flame and smoke belched out from the windows. It was a grand but horrifying sight.

The burned-out buildings I saw stretched out along the street that ran north to south were like ribs on the vertebra of some modern monster. I stood riveted to the spot, fascinated by what one could perhaps call the "monstrous magnificence" of it all. The rows of large ghostly "tombstones" I had seen from the top of Hijiyama Hill were these very buildings.

The streets were littered with enormous numbers of dead bodies and remnants of vehicles. But I had gradually become less sensitive to those things. And by now my prohibitions were becoming second nature to me. That's probably why I was able to linger a while and take in the scenes of stark desolation in the heart of this incinerated city.

I started wondering whether I should go straight home to Funairi by way of Aioi Bridge or whether I should stop off first at the university via Takanohashi. Soon, however, I found myself walking in the direction of Takanohashi. The "monstrous magnificence" had me in its grip.

—December 10, 1945

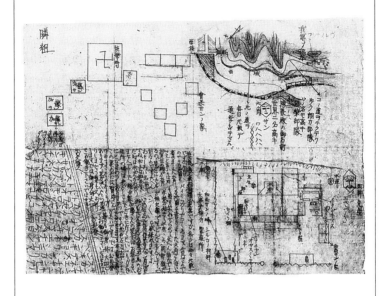

In this letter to her parents, eleven-year-old Kazuko includes drawings showing the layout of the temple and the relation of the building to the surrounding farmhouses. She includes, at bottom left, a brief note written entirely in the Japanese alphabet, without Chinese characters, to her younger brother, Kinji. (NOTE: The reverse swastika is an ancient Buddhist symbol. A translation of this letter appears on page 186.)

Mothers and Children

August 6, 1945

Fumiyo,

I headed south from Kamiyacho toward Shiragami Shrine. As I passed by Kokutaiji Temple, I was shocked to see that the big camphor tree that had been designated a natural monument had been incinerated, as had the residence of the nineteenth-century writer and historian, Rai Sanyo. Nothing was left at the temple but tombstones. I was walking along, staring blankly at the transformed scenery, when I heard a woman's voice.

"Hello there. I see that you're all right. And how is Mrs. Ogura?"

Turning in the direction of the voice, I saw your former tea ceremony and flower arrangement teacher, who'd been to our house several times in the past. I couldn't recall her name but I knew her from her aristocratic nose, even though I could barely see it as she was swathed in bandages from the top of her head to her throat. She was wearing a dark blue men's suit jacket, whitish *monpe* work pants and rubber-soled footwear. Her left arm was bandaged.

She told me she'd gone to an area south of the Red Cross Hospital to take part in some house demolition work. Just as she'd stooped down to begin working, there was a brilliant flash and she'd lost consciousness. When she came to, she found herself buried to her waist in debris. Through a haze of yellowish smoke—

it must have been dust—she could see figures lying here and there on the ground. She struggled free, stood up and looked around, but she couldn't see anyone else who was still alive, anywhere around her.

She'd started running before she knew what she was doing. When she finally paused to catch her breath, she was at the west end of Miyuki Bridge.

It was there that she realized that she was naked from the waist up. Her blouse was gone and only its elastic waistband remained. She suddenly felt very embarrassed. Just then she saw a men's suit jacket, abandoned, lying on the streetcar line right before her eyes. She picked it up and put it on. "This is it," she said with a rueful smile, raising both her arms slightly.

She'd then crossed Miyuki Bridge and run in the direction of Hijiyama Hill. On the way, she came to a rescue station near where either the teacher's college or the army signal corps had been, she wasn't exactly sure. She waited a while and had a bandage applied to her left arm, which was bleeding. It seems that a piece of broken lumber had pierced her skin. The attendants had just dabbed the wound with some antiseptic before applying the bandage. They then told her that she had burns too, from her head down to her shoulders, so they applied bandages all around her head and face. After that the burns began to tingle and smart.

As the afternoon wore on, more and more people arrived at the rescue station, she said. She heard that the streets of the city were passable, and even though her burns were hurting badly, she decided to walk to her married daughter's home in Ushida. She was given a lift partway on a truck bound for Koi, and had gotten off a short while before we met. She said she planned to get to her daughter's house by walking across the West Parade Ground. You once said that she was a courageous woman. And to travel that far alone in these circumstances seemed to me indeed to require courage.

Just then a shrill, quavering cry filled the afternoon air. We both turned and saw a woman, barefoot, her hair disheveled, wearing nothing but a pair of *monpe* work pants, running toward us from the direction of Otemachi. She passed quite close by and ran across the streetcar lines toward Takeyacho Street, weeping and screaming maniacally.

"It's her again!" your teacher exclaimed, startled.

I watched speechlessly as the apparition-like image receded into the flickering ruins. Your tea ceremony teacher said that she'd seen the very same woman running toward Otemachi earlier, as she was climbing off the truck. She surmised that the woman must have lost her child in the blast. She'd seen several such women at the rescue station. Without seeming to take any notice of their own, often serious, injuries they howled and screamed as if possessed for the children they'd lost.

The teacher left then, but I stood for a while looking alternately after the deranged woman and the figure of your teacher. I was filled with a keen awareness of the intensity of the bond between a mother and her child. I began to think that rather than being purely spiritual in nature, such feelings seem to have physiological and primitive or even animalistic origins. Even now, I can clearly recall that encounter with the poor creature. Thinking of it always makes me wonder if my own parental instinct will be strong enough for me to raise our three children alone.

I saw many other people just like your teacher, badly injured but plodding painfully along, probably intent on getting to the homes of relatives in the suburbs. They all shuffled along sluggishly, as if in a trance. Trucks carrying similarly injured people were everywhere, as were trucks filled with corpses.

Near Takanohashi too, there were many such trucks, heading for Ujina, Koi and Hijiyama Hill. The whole area had been destroyed by fire, with only the burned-out structures of our university, the Red Cross Hospital and the Postal Service Bureau building still standing in a row like the odd remaining teeth in an otherwise completely decayed mouth.

I entered the university grounds through the gate of the national middle school affiliated with the teachers' college. The campus was strangely quiet. As I'd observed from the top of Hijiyama Hill, only the ferroconcrete shells of the university's main building and the national school were still standing. The teacher's college and the buildings around it had been reduced to ashes. Only the chimney of the dormitory dining hall was still standing, and it looked as if it were surveying the ruins. The building between the university and the middle school, where the portraits of the emperor and empress were housed,* was the only one to escape damage altogether. I assumed that the university officials must have been relieved, anyway, about that. However, the sturdy-looking steel doors had been bowed deeply inward by the force of the blast.

The pumpkin and sweet potato vines that had been planted throughout the open area in front of the main university building lay torn up and scattered all over the grounds. The leaves were scorched a reddish brown. Across the open area, the large posts of the front gate, the library warehouse and the weapons storehouse were still standing.**

All my belongings, and all those of the students assigned to accompany me to the factory, had been placed for safekeeping in the weapons storehouse. They were to have been taken over to the factory by truck the next day. I was about to look inside the storehouse, when I spotted Professor Watanabe standing near the air-raid shelter with a few other people, and went over to speak with him. Professor Watanabe is a very good, conscientious man and serves as chief of air-raid precautions for the entire university and the associated complex. With him were a couple of clerks and a young naval officer. The officer was from the Kure district naval headquarters, which had been using part of the university

---

* [Through the end of World War II, every school, college and university received such portraits from the government, together with an imperial rescript on education proclaimed by Emperor Meiji. The schools were duty bound to safeguard these items.]

** [Prior to and during World War II, students from middle school through university levels were required to take part in military drills. Weapons for student practice use were stored on the school grounds.]

building for its research. Professor Watanabe and the people with him were the only personnel left on campus. All the other teachers, students and employees who were there at the time of the blast had either been taken off to the hospital or had gone to seek refuge elsewhere.

Two or three pumpkins lay on the ground near the air-raid shelter and pieces of pumpkin skin were strewn around the spot. The pumpkins had been baked by ambient heat where they lay on the ground.

"They're delicious. You should try one," said Professor Watanabe.

I split one open and tasted it. It was surprisingly good. Realizing I hadn't had any lunch, I glanced at my watch and saw it was five o'clock already. I suddenly felt hungry, but I didn't feel like eating the lunch I had been carrying with me all day. So I had a whole pumpkin by myself—a rather large one too. You loved pumpkins, didn't you?

I talked with Professor Watanabe for a while and then went to the entrance hall of the main university building. On the half-open steel door was a notice written in a bold hand with chalk: "The orders of the Vice Governor shall be followed henceforth. August 6—Chugoku District Government." Alongside it was another, in Professor Watanabe's handwriting, that read: "The university's main building was totally destroyed by fire at 12:30— Chief of Air-Raid Precautions." Regarding the other notice, as I mentioned earlier, the Chugoku district government had been occupying the third floor of the main building. In the reshuffling that had been done to accommodate them, I had been assigned a new office on the ground floor off the entrance hallway. Naturally, I wanted to see what state the room was in, so I went over that way first. The bookshelves, desks, chairs and everything else had been incinerated. The room was like a big furnace, scattered with residual fires still burning and glowing embers. In the corridor too, the ceiling had dropped down and the side walls had collapsed, creating piles of rubble that were still smoldering. I turned and ran outside. I said goodbye to Professor Watanabe and headed toward the main gate.

I stopped on my way out and saw that the weapons storehouse—and the library warehouse as well—was completely burned out, just as I had feared.

The fire had spared the Red Cross Hospital directly opposite the gate, and I thought I'd go by to see some injured colleagues Professor Watanabe had mentioned. The area from the gate to the main hospital entrance was simply packed with people with all kinds of burns and injuries. I tried to ease my way around them and finally managed to reach the door. Still more people were crowded inside. Some were sprawled or squatting on the floor; others waited for treatment while standing in queues that zigged and zagged. White-gowned doctors and nurses were trying to move carefully through the throngs. I soon realized this was no time to be looking for anyone, so I left. I've subsequently learned from other people of things that happened at this hospital that day. Since you were familiar with the place, I'll write more about them later.

The devastation between the streetcar stops for the university and Takanohashi was really shocking. The coffee shop, bookstore, secondhand bookstore, watch shop, photo studio, stationery store, shoe store and all the places that used to line both sides of the street—I can vividly recall the displays, the faces of the clerks, even the locations where people usually stood in each shop—had disappeared and been replaced by large mounds of still-flickering embers arranged in neat rows along the thoroughfare.

I found myself looking for the remains of the photographic supply shop, Yagi Tonbodo, which you also knew very well. Whenever my assistants or I needed any help with photographs necessary for our research, we always went first to that store. The proprietor was such a kind elderly gentleman, and we were on such friendly terms with him that we thought of him as a technical member of our research department. He and his equally pleasant wife were a contented old couple, like a modern version of the Noh play, *The Old Couple of Takasago.* I couldn't help feeling that he would suddenly emerge, smiling, from his darkroom, his bald head shining. But I was unable even to locate the spot where his shop had stood.

Later, when temporary shops started to spring up in the area, none was erected that displayed the "Tonbodo" sign. Survivors who'd been in the vicinity at the time said that the elderly couple had probably died when the flames took their building, which had collapsed. I made inquiries, but no one knew what happened to their remains. I believe they'd left their hometowns in Shikoku when they were quite young and that they had no children. So perhaps urns containing their ashes are lying around somewhere, unclaimed. However, if they really did die together, as some believe, they must have died happy. At least that's what I'd like to believe.

When I reached Takanohashi, the sun was well over to the west and I realized for the first time that dusk was coming on rapidly. Since morning, when I'd climbed to the top of Hijiyama Hill, the sun had been like a dark red copper disk, its circumference blurred yellow as if ringed with a phantom corona. It had been gloomy, as if a solar eclipse were in progress. Now the sun shone clearer, probably because the fires and smoke had abated.

At Takanohashi, I picked up my pace like a mechanical doll someone had just remembered to rewind. Dead bodies and electric wires lay everywhere on the streets. There were quite a few people coming into the city from the suburbs on bicycles and on foot. They had apparently come to look for relatives or friends. There were also endless streams of injured people like your teacher, probably trying to make their way to relatives' or friends' houses. There were many trucks on the road as well. I went as fast as I could, picking my way through the pedestrians and vehicles.

I can hardly recall what I saw or heard around there. But I do remember that there were a number of corpses drifting down the river and that small boats with outboard motors, referred to locally as *yanma*, were hauling them out of the water. I heard later that bodies found in the waters of the estuary down around Ujina were picked up and taken to nearby Ninoshima Island, where they were cremated or buried.

Just as I'd crossed the bridge, I saw another woman who was clearly very disconcerted and agitated. She was some distance away but judging from her clothing, she looked Korean. She was making a cry that sounded like *Aigo! Aigo!* and would every so often violently beat the piles of ashes around her with what looked like a thick bamboo rod. She eventually shouldered the rod and went on her way. I could see that the end of the rod was all shredded and that it swayed, catching the light of the setting sun as she walked.

I couldn't go much faster.

The area from Meiji Bridge to Sumiyoshi Bridge had been destroyed by fire. Only the high walls of Hiroshima Prison to the left were still standing; there was no sign of fire or smoke beyond them. Dead bodies floated along in the river on either side of Sumiyoshi Bridge. When I reached the other side of the bridge, there was nothing but burned wasteland all around me. There was no doubt about it now, I thought. Our house must definitely have burned down.

I came to the main street where the streetcars ran, and turned left. The hills of Eba appeared in front of me. This area too was a sea of cinders and ashes that stretched toward the hills. I couldn't even locate the road on the right that went past our house. Then I noticed what looked like a long row of corpses laid out side by side along the streetcar line. When I went to have a closer look, I found that they were not corpses, but people who were badly injured or burned. A horrible chorus of cries and groans filled the air.

"It hurts!"

"I want some water!"

"Mother!"

But spare me the pain, Fumiyo, of telling you any more details about those poor souls. The scene made me quite nervous. It was a few minutes before I managed to get my emotions under control and started scrutinizing the victims. There were a lot of other people there looking them over as well. It was just like being at the fish market. I checked every single one of the victims and was relieved when I couldn't find anyone remotely resembling you or Kinji.

"No. They're not here," one person said to another searching nearby.

"They probably fled toward Koi," came the response. This exchange made me wonder if maybe you and Kinji hadn't also headed toward Koi.

Anyone could see there was not much hope for these wounded. No one was receiving any actual medical treatment. Crude cubicles had been erected using remnants of doors and panels that had not burned, making this look like a casualty treatment station, though it was really nothing more than a temporary repository.

I learned later that at almost all the rescue stations priority was placed on treating only those people whose injuries were quickly judged to be less severe, while those whose cases were considered hopeless were just left unattended. So even if injured people did manage to drag themselves to rescue stations, they had to join others in long queues; many didn't survive long enough to receive treatment. I suppose this was unavoidable under the circumstances. Most hospitals had been incinerated and nearly all the doctors and nurses had been killed or wounded.

I later heard a student tell a story about a little girl he saw at one rescue station. The place was so inundated with people that a decision was made to separate the mortally wounded from the others and leave them, untreated. However, one little girl of five or six, whose injuries were only slight, refused to leave the side of her grievously wounded mother. A station attendant reluctantly pulled the screaming child away and dragged her toward the other queue. "But she's alive!" the child wailed.

I saw a similar scene myself here among the rows of living dead.

Having satisfied myself that neither you nor Kinji were there,

I was about to go when a small boy, about three or four, came toddling along carrying a small can of water. He looked like he was playing house or something. He trotted up to the head of one of the "living corpses" near where I was standing, squatted down and started pouring the water into the person's mouth. When the can was empty, he stood up and went off to fill it again. At the time, water was still flowing out of broken pipes and faucets all over the devastated area. The child was probably getting the water from one of those sources. The victim was a woman. She lay face up and had a black sash, the kind used for carrying small children, crossed over her breast. At one point, she must have had the little boy strapped to her back. I noticed that her light summer blouse was drenched with blood, from her left shoulder down to her chest. Looking closer, I saw that her left arm was torn away at the shoulder. The wound looked like a ripe fig split open. She seemed, in fact, to be already dead. Her eyes were closed and her face was pale and rigid. The water which the little boy poured into her mouth would just spill over onto her throat and bosom, diluting the blood on her clothing. It might have been her voice I'd heard before, pleading for water. I watched the little boy go away once more, looking happy enough. I didn't want to be there when he came back so I averted my gaze and started walking.

I found a narrow alley going to the right. As I turned down it, I recognized it as the one that went past our house. Your brother's house had collapsed and then burned. Turning to the left, I walked further down the alley. I looked for our house but all I could see were piles of broken roof tiles and burned lumber. The slightly higher pile of debris near the entrance to the alley was definitely the remnants of your brother's two-storey house, while the smaller pile next to it must have been ours. The embers were still burning and sending up ribbons of smoke. Pieces of collapsed walls lined both sides of the narrow alley like the banks of a river, leaving just enough space for me to walk down the alleyway to our property.

There was no one around. The cistern in front of our house containing water for fire emergencies was intact and full. The goldfish was swimming around inside it.* It was definitely alive. In fact it was the only living, moving thing that I could see around the place. I don't know how long I stood there absentmindedly looking at it, watching it open and close its mouth in rapid gulping motions.

"They probably fled toward Koi." The conversation I'd overheard earlier sprang to mind again, and I wondered whether you and Kinji had indeed gone toward Koi.

I started walking briskly out of the alley. I turned left as I emerged and soon came to the site of Funairi Hospital. This area too was devastated by fire. Turning right off the road on the river embankment, I came to Kan'on Bridge, which I crossed. Another desolate expanse, this one extending to Nishi-ohashi Bridge, came into view. As I approached the bridge, loose pumpkin vines that the blast had blown onto the road from nearby gardens kept winding about my feet. I crossed this bridge too and found that the area beyond it had not been damaged by fire—only the slaughterhouse had been destroyed.

Once across the Asahi Bridge, I came to Koi Station on the Miyajima Line. Though the station was badly damaged, it hadn't burned. But the houses all around it and the other station, right in front of it, which served the government railroad, were gone. Areas further beyond, though, seemed to have escaped the conflagration. The dark green hills in the background looked quiet and peaceful.

The sun was now almost hidden by the hills.

The Miyajima Line was not running. I went over to the government railroad station but the trains there too were stopped. So you and Kinji couldn't have gone to Jigozen, I thought, since it was a good twelve kilometers southwest of here.

We had lived in Koi once for a while, so I suddenly started to

---

* [Fish were kept in these vessels to prevent mosquitoes from breeding.]

think that maybe you and Kinji had gone to stay with one of our old acquaintances in the area. I was thinking specifically of our friends Takeo and Chiyo Yamanaka, though the husband, Takeo, was away in the army, or Tadajiro Yamaoka, our former landlord.

First, I went to Mr. Yamaoka's, as it was the closer from the station.

Though the Koi area had thankfully escaped the ravages of fire, houses there had still been badly damaged. The damage was a lot worse than it had been around Aiko's. In particular, the greenhouses that were a common sight around Koi were obliterated. Glass fragments dotted the neighboring fields like unseasonable flowers made of ice.

Although Mr. Yamaoka's own house was still standing, as was the one he rented out, the roof tiles and all the doors and screens had been blasted off. Still, the whole family was safe. I asked about you and Kinji but they didn't know anything. Mr. Yamaoka said he'd just come from the rescue station that had been established at the national school, but that he hadn't seen you or Kinji there. He kindly volunteered to go back there with me to look for you.

You know the Koi national school very well, but you wouldn't have recognized it. The big school yard, the gym, the classrooms, the corridors were all filled to overflowing with rows of mortally wounded victims, just like I'd seen at the rescue station on the streetcar lines at Funairi. The large objects lying in the school yard, covered with coarse straw mats, were corpses. The evening air, inside and outside the buildings, was thick with the smell of death. There must have been hundreds of dead and dying there.

Mr. Yamaoka and I split up and went systemically down the rows, walking first among the living victims, scrutinizing each face. When we came to the corpses, we lifted the straw mats, one after another. Eventually, when it grew quite dark, Mr. Yamaoka borrowed a paper lantern from somewhere and together we continued searching for you among all those faces by the weak glow of candlelight.

It makes me shudder now, when I think back on the way I was able to view everything with an air of utter detachment.

Mr. Yamaoka and I searched the school grounds very thoroughly but naturally we didn't find you or Kinji.

He took me to the makeshift office that the rescue station had established in the school building. We were handed some loose sheets of paper containing the names and addresses of wounded people who'd been brought in. We were told that some of the victims listed there had since been transferred to other places, so we divided the lists between us and looked them over carefully. They had apparently been examined by countless others too because the penciled names and addresses were so smudged and soiled. It was hard to read them by candlelight, but we persisted, and finally had read all the names.

"They aren't here," I said.

Mr. Yamaoka said nothing. He probably didn't know what to say. I thanked him for his help and said I'd go on then to the Yamanakas', to see if you and Kinji were there. He kindly suggested that I spend the night at his house. I realized for the first time that I had nowhere to stay and that I couldn't very well ask Chiyo to put me up when Takeo was away. So I gratefully accepted, telling him I'd return to his house later that night, after stopping by the Yamanakas'.

As you know, their house was two-storeyed and built on a hill. It looked like the house had been badly damaged but in the dark it was hard to tell the exact extent of the damage. A dim light was just visible from the kitchen. I knew the layout of the house, and went around to the back entrance. Furniture and kitchen utensils lay scattered everywhere. Chiyo was sitting on the wooden floor, in a small space she'd made by pushing aside broken tiles and hunks of plaster. She was sitting alone, a candle burning beside her. She looked very dejected and was apparently wearing the clothes she'd on when the blast occurred. She told me that the upstairs part of the house had been totally destroyed and that this was the only spot where she could rest. Her husband had been called up for military service in the Philippines and she'd had no word from him. Their two children had been evacuated, together with their classmates, to remote parts of the country. Seeing a young woman all alone like this, in such dire straits, left me at a complete loss for words.

Chiyo had no idea where you were either. She'd gone off to Dobashi that morning, assigned, like many others, to house demolition work. When she got to the site, she didn't feel well, so she decided to return home. She was knocked to the ground by the blast on her way back. She was not hurt, but no one in her entire work group survived. She said she couldn't help feeling guilty about that. I uttered some words of encouragement and left.

As you know, you can see the entire city of Hiroshima from Takeo and Chiyo's. All over, residual fires were still burning. The sensation of looking down into a volcanic crater was further enhanced now by the dark. In particular, the juxtaposition of the brightness of the Milky Way and the other stars in the night sky with the fiery ruins below gave such an impression of primordial grandeur it almost made me forget my worries about you and Kinji.

It must have been about nine o'clock when I got back to the Yamaokas'. Mrs. Yamaoka kindly made me some supper. There were three other people eating in the dim candlelight, and we took turns recounting what we had seen and experienced during the day. The others had come to the city for the day from the countryside. They were being put up for the night by the Yamaokas because train and bus service was at a standstill, making it impossible for them to go home. Fortunately, none was seriously injured, and they all told their stories with a lot of energy. I listened without saying much myself. No one's account differed greatly from what I'd experienced during the day.

But then Mr. Yamaoka said, "When the black rain started to fall …"

"Eh?" I couldn't help exclaiming. Two of the others also looked at him with surprise.

"I was in Yokogawa when it fell," the third man said. "I was terrified. I thought it was some kind of incendiary bomb that sprayed oil."

Mr. Yamaoka said he guessed the black rain had started about an hour after the explosion, but I know now that that's not quite correct. Some people told me later it started shortly after the explosion, like a squall of pitch-black rain. It seems that soot, ash and dust, rising into the atmosphere, had mingled with the rain that fell right after the explosion. The black rain also contained vast quantities of scorched fabric and other solid materials that fell to the ground or stuck to the skin, so some thought that this meant the rumored oil-based incendiary bomb had been dropped. Judging from later reports, the black rain seems to have fallen mostly in the western half of Hiroshima and the area extending from Yokogawa to the valley district a few kilometers beyond. They say it stemmed from meteorological changes in the atmosphere caused by the bomb. So, the "pageant of clouds" I'd seen in the morning had been accompanied, in some places, by black rain.

Mr. Yamaoka had been in a reclaimed area near the sea at the time of the explosion. He was hurled into a soybean field by the force of the blast but was not hurt. He stood up and looked over toward the embankment. Some of the people who'd been riding their bicycles along it a moment before had been thrown—with their bicycles—onto the opposite slope of the embankment. I thought of the man with the deformed bicycle I'd seen that morning.

Finally, the discussion came around to the question of what had actually happened. Eyes turned in my direction—no doubt because I was a university professor, and local people sometimes expected us to know everything. I was about to say that it was probably an atomic bomb when I realized I didn't know enough about it to explain it to anyone. Besides, I was also very tired. So I said I had no idea what had happened, but that it must have been some completely new kind of weapon.

Later, we pulled away enough debris to make a space to sleep in, and set up a large mosquito net. We all crept under and went to bed side by side, in the clothes we were wearing.

When the candles were extinguished, we could see a dim glow coming from the direction of Hiroshima. Lying on my back, I could see stars twinkling in the sky through the net and the big holes in the roof where tiles had been ripped away. The breathing of the others grew steady, but I couldn't seem to fall asleep.

Each time I started to doze off, I would see deranged women emerging from fiery ruins, the faces of armless mothers, charred corpses of little children, but especially the little boy trotting off to get water for his dead mother. I'd then see you and Kinji in the same situation. All I could think about were the figures of mothers and children I'd seen that day, and then these would turn into visions of you and Kinji. Finally I fell into a deep sleep.

—December 21, 1945

6

Continuing the Search

August 7, 1945

Fumiyo,

The next day, August 7, dawned clear. The midsummer sun shone brightly, in contrast with the day before, when smoke had completely blotted out the light.

But I was more despondent than ever. Uncertain whether I'd ever find you or Kinji alive, or if I'd even be able to retrieve your bodies, I had a tasteless breakfast. The other three people who had stayed overnight at the Yamaokas' soon left, at which point Mr. Yamaoka brought a ladder around from the back of the house, saying that he was going to fix the roof. I hadn't noticed it before, but the tatami mats and the furniture were badly soiled by the "black rain" that had fallen the night before, and were still wet.

I chose to leave at that time as well, and to try once more to find you in the Koi area, this time by asking people if they'd seen either of you. And I resolved that whether I was successful or not, I would go on in the afternoon to the factory where I was assigned for the day.

First I headed back to the national school. On the way, I ran into several of your acquaintances whom I knew by sight but not by name. I asked each of them whether they knew where you or Kinji were, but no one did. In the school yard I ran into our dear old friend, Mr. Matsuki.

"You must be very worried about your family," he said sympathetically. He had run into Mr. Yamaoka the night before and heard about our situation.

The number of corpses laid out in the school yard had risen dramatically since the previous evening, and they were no longer covered with straw mats. Many of the dead were children of middle-school age, boys and girls alike. All had been burned terribly. The boys had been wearing only trousers; many boys' were in tatters. The girls' blouses were scorched and stuck to the skin in patches. Many girls wore *monpe* pants that were sliced to ribbons; others only had on underwear.

"Some of them kept calling for their mothers in the night," Mr. Matsuki told me.

Most of these children had been creating firebreaks near the Dobashi and Honkawa bridges. Since the houses in the area had been pulled down, the children were working in groups with nothing to shield them when the flash occurred. Not only did they sustain severe burns, but they were literally thrown to the ground by the force of the blast. Many died where they fell. Those who managed to make their way to the school yard before dying were perhaps more fortunate than the others, many of whom were virtually cremated on the spot. Quite a few must have died trying to get back to the school.

Many adult bodies also lay in the school yard. Some of these were the teachers who were in charge at the time of the flash. I was deeply moved to hear that teachers had asked rescue personnel to attend to the children first. I learned later that Professor Kurita's daughter, who worked at the First Girls' High School, was one of the teachers who had made this request.

"In any case, the children who died here stand a good chance of being identified and claimed by their parents, and of their souls ascending to the pure land of merciful Amitabha," Mr. Matsuki said quietly, almost to himself. He was a firm believer in the Pure Land sect of Buddhism.

He turned to me and said, "Don't lose heart, Mr. Ogura. I'm sure you'll find them."

He left then, chanting the Amida Buddha's name in a low tone.

As you know, the students aged about fifteen and older who were in the third year of middle school or above had been mobilized for work in factories and other locations. The children who had been making firebreaks were all about thirteen or fourteen years old; they included first- and second-year middle school students as well as students at the higher national schools. National school students, aged about eight to twelve, had been evacuated in groups to outlying areas, where they lived with their teachers. Smaller children were at home with their parents until after second grade, when they would likely move to the countryside.

I found out later that the most tragic victims of the bombing were the members of volunteer work groups engaged in this particular work. All such job sites were located in the center of the city and many people had been working stripped to the waist in the midsummer sun when the flash occurred. Aiko's father-in-law and your brother Tetsuji Tanaka's mother-in-law, who were both working in such groups at the time, were among the missing. Although no human lives are worth more than others, the deaths of groups of young children are perhaps the most heartrending.

After Mr. Matsuki left, I turned back to the task of trying to find you. Familiar now with the layout of the school from the night before, I started searching the yard and the building once more, going up and down the rows of mortally wounded and dead. The stench was stronger now than the night before; it even irritated my eyes. My ears were inured to people's cries and pleas, although the voices of children calling out for their mothers made me very angry.

Fancy mobilizing babies like these, I thought.

I left and went on to the part of Koi where we used to live. I went door-to-door asking about you, but to no avail. I decided then to go back to the site of our house in Funairi.

From Asahi Bridge to Nishi-ohashi Bridge, and from there to Kan'on Bridge—that's the only route you could have taken, seeking refuge. I was so sure of this that I didn't consider any other routes. So with the early morning sun beating down as it had the day before, I went back along that same route, carefully inspecting each corpse I came across, till I reached the burned-out ruins of our home. Near the site of our house lay the charred and contorted corpse of a child, in a posture similar to one that Kinji used to assume in the "dance" he'd perform after dinner to make us laugh. Startled, I went closer and leaned over. The face was charred black—I couldn't identify it. But it definitely wasn't Kinji.

In the alley, I came upon a group of four or five people, clearly from the neighborhood, who were staring glassy-eyed at the burning debris and muttering amongst themselves. As you know, I was not very familiar with our neighbors because we'd only recently moved to this part of Hiroshima and I was rarely at home. But they apparently knew who I was, because one of them said, "You must be very worried about your family."

I asked about you and Kinji, but they all said they hadn't seen you the morning before. The only thing I did learn from them was that you had not taken part in the voluntary work scheduled for that day.

The thought kept recurring that perhaps you had both been trapped and burned to death beneath the house. But the heat of the embers had not yet subsided, and I couldn't even approach the spot where our house had stood. I would have to wait another two or three days before I could look.

It was also very possible that you and Kinji had managed to escape from the burning house, but had later died from your injuries.

Or you may both have escaped unscathed. But since I hadn't found any trace of you in Koi, this was unlikely. And I couldn't imagine that you might have reached Jigozen, when the trains were not running.

I went back to the same makeshift rescue station on the streetcar lines that I had passed through the day before. I searched carefully, but in vain. This time I did not see the mother with the missing arm, or her little boy. After a little while, I found myself walking on Kan'on Bridge, heading back toward Koi; I must literally have been sleepwalking. Anyway, I arrived back in Koi again, though I don't remember crossing Asahi Bridge. It was nearly eleven o'clock in the morning. I remembered once more that I was supposed to go to the factory, but now it didn't bother me so much. I was very tired and growing resigned to the situation.

I went to see how things were at the Koi government railroad station. The trains were still not running. The streetcars too were at a standstill, so there was no choice but to walk. I recalled the route I'd taken the previous day. The shortest way back would be to retrace that route or walk straight along the streetcar tracks. I certainly didn't feel like walking through that blackened wreckage again. But the hope and confidence I'd had about finding you had dulled somewhat and my feelings had grown a bit numb. I supposed I'd be able to pass by those corpses without giving them so much as a glance.

So I started walking along the railroad track from the burned station platform. Soon the Koi town line was behind me and I came to the place where the Chausu Hill slopes into the Yamate River, leaving an area just wide enough to accommodate the railroad and the narrow roadway.

From around there, you recall, you could only see the western part of Hiroshima. Now I could take in the whole city. Hijiyama Hill and the houses still standing around Minamicho, just outside the blackened area, also appeared much closer than they did before.

I was beginning to feel hungry, and thought I'd look for a place to sit on the dry riverbed of the Yamate River and eat some of the bread I'd been carrying around with me since the day before. I saw someone lying on the grassy strip adjoining the riverbed, near where we used to bring the children on outings. For a minute I thought this person had stopped here, as I had, to have lunch, and was taking a nap after his meal. But on closer inspection, I found that he was not sleeping, but dead. Then I

looked about and saw more bodies everywhere, not only on the
grassy strip, but also on the white sand of the riverbed. The black
dots in the fields on the other side of the river looked like corpses
too. No doubt all these burned and injured people had hoped to
reach the water and quench their raging thirst.

I couldn't be sure you and Kinji were not among them.

But there would be no end to it if I extended my search across
the river. Besides, I thought I'd have only the slimmest chance of
finding you and Kinji there. So I gave up the idea and proceeded
bleakly on my way. My appetite of course had disappeared.

Crossing over the railroad bridge from Yamatecho and approaching Uchikoshicho, I saw dead bodies under the bridge, on the
tracks, on the slopes of the riverbanks and in the vegetable gardens on both sides of the bridge. But the area just beyond, where
the hills began, was not burned. These people must have been
fleeing from fire, running toward the tree-covered hills when they
finally succumbed to their injuries. Many of the corpses lay stiffly
in postures that suggested that they had been walking or running
when they collapsed and died. In a cornfield I saw a corpse held
upright by the stalks, looking like a statue of a sportsman in
action. At least these people must have died with their eyes fixed
on the green mountainside.

The part of Uchikoshicho that faced onto Yokogawa was
burned. Yokogawa Station was a shambles and Yokogawacho, south
of the station, had of course been destroyed by fire. The burned areas
extended a considerable distance into Misasacho and Kusunokicho,
north of the railroad. If Hijiyama Hill is taken as the southeastern
edge of the fires, then Misacho and Kusunokicho should probably
be regarded as the northwestern limit. The area from Nakahirocho
to Hirosecho and Nishiteramachi was also largely consumed and
the tiled roofs of the big Buddhist temples of Teramachi were
gone. To my great sorrow, the gigantic main building of the
Hiroshima Honganji Temple, which had previously been visible
from any point in the area and served as a visual counterbalance
to Hiroshima Castle, was no longer there.

I went east a little ways from Yokogawa Station and came to the railroad bridge at Misasa. Hakushima and the surrounding areas across the river were a sea of ruins. The cherry trees in the Chojuen Gardens had been severely battered but the fires had spared the army engineering regimental area upstream. I was about to walk across the badly wrecked railroad bridge when I decided that it would be easier to make my way by walking next to the road. So I walked downstream for a while along the river embankment, and came to Misasa Bridge.

When I started across it, I was surprised to find that the entire low concrete wall on the south side had fallen, neatly, onto the pedestrian path of the bridge. There was no trace of the north-side wall. Looking down into the river on that side, I then saw it lying deep in the water below. The south-side parapet—made of thick concrete—had been shoved over about one meter to the north before it had collapsed onto the path. This was the first time I'd seen such undeniable physical evidence of the force of the blast.

The walls of Tokiwa Bridge in Nigitsu were dislodged and destroyed in much the same manner. I learned later that practically all the bridges that stood perpendicular to the general direction of the blast and which were within about two kilometers of the center of the explosion had suffered the same fate. Even the long, solid walls of Miyuki Bridge, further still from the explosion, collapsed in a clean, unbroken line. But all the bridges that were more or less parallel to the blast, even those less than two kilometers away, were virtually undamaged. I was amazed by the geometric consistency of the destructive force.

When I got to Hakushima, I was astonished to see that Hiroshima Castle had disappeared. Actually, I had thought it strange that I couldn't see the castle from Yokogawa Station. The only remaining traces of it were small mounds of burned lumber on top of elevated stone foundations. The various army buildings that had stood in the area must have been incinerated too. Only the brick side walls of the army cadet preparatory school were standing, looking like ancient Roman ruins.

You know how the railroad bridge and Tokiwa Bridge cross over the middle of the part of the river that's shaped like an inverted *s*? Well, there is a fairly wide sandbar upstream on the Hakushima side, and another downstream on the Nigitsu side. As you know, Sentei Park is a little further downstream. The sandbar below was littered with dead bodies. I also saw some corpses floating in the water just below the bridge.

I was accustomed to scenes like that from the day before, but a row of burned-out freight cars standing on the upstream railroad bridge was new to me. They were probably passing over the bridge just as the flash occurred. Looking past the bridge, I could see a crowd of people gathered on the wide sandbar upstream. That was probably the one safe haven available to inhabitants of the area from Higashi-hakushima to Kyukencho, just as Hijiyama Hill was to people in the eastern part of the city.

I was gazing off toward the sandbar, wondering if conditions were as bad there as they had been on Hijiyama Hill when I heard someone call out to me. I turned around and saw Ikushima, a former university student of mine, who lived nearby. His house, which had stood on the riverbank near the upstream sandbar, had collapsed and burned, he told me. He and his wife had fled to the sandbar, where they'd been staying. Both had escaped serious injury, but Ikushima's aged father had been trapped beneath the house, and they had had to leave him to a fiery death.

While we were talking, Kondo, another former student who'd graduated about the same time as Ikushima, came along. He was living in Nagaregawa and had been trapped when his house had collapsed in the blast. He struggled frantically to free himself and had finally managed to scramble out through the roof that had fallen onto him. He made a desperate attempt to rescue his family from under the debris but the house was enveloped in flames too quickly. He had fled alone to Sentei Park. The park had served as a refuge for local people until the fires reached it. At that point Kondo had jumped into the Kanda River and then waded across to Nigitsu and stayed at a friend's in Ushida. Thinking that the fires must have subsided, he was heading back to try to retrieve his family's remains. He said that only the southwestern part of Ushida, facing the Kanda River, had been burned. I then told them about the experiences I had had till then.

We stood together on the bridge for some time, looking off toward the city. Columns of black smoke still rose everywhere from the embers. We made halfhearted attempts to cheer each other up before smiling wanly and going our separate ways. From the western end of the bridge, I watched the two young men, one heading northerly and the other southward, until both disappeared from sight. Then I went east across the bridge. Their forced smiles stayed with me long afterward. I'm sure mine seemed just as hollow to them.

The two big restaurant buildings on the east side of Tokiwa Bridge had been badly damaged by fire. When I passed under the railroad bridge, I saw that the Nigitsu Shrine, the trees in the park and Tsuruhane Shrine, where we'd held our wedding ceremony, had all burned down. The leaves of the trees on Mount Futaba were now a reddish brown, like those on Hijiyama Hill. Corpses, many of them soldiers', lined the roads from Tokiwa Bridge to Nigitsu.

I also noticed that the facilities of the Second Army Headquarters had been reduced to ashes. The burned remains of the roadside monument to fallen military horses still stood, though.

Several rescue stations now stood on the army's vast East Parade Ground, drawing large crowds of people seeking shelter or medical attention. I learned later that members of Kure's navy medical service corps had come to the East Parade Ground soon after the bombing to handle rescue operations.

I walked east along the northern edge of the parade ground and managed to get to Onagacho. The national school and the Matsumoto Commercial School had been razed by fire, but areas further east were not burned. This part of the city was apparently the northeastern boundary of the fires that had swept Hiroshima. When I realized I had at last gotten out of the annihilated area, I was overcome by a deep fatigue. My watch said that it was nearly two and I was desperate now to get to the factory. I somehow managed to reach the dormitory office of Nippon Steel's Funakoshi factory about an hour later.

The students were supposed to assemble at three o'clock but only two or three had turned up. Professors Shirai and Doi, who were to supervise with me, were not there either. By early evening, only ten students had arrived. Some who were living there and were now serving as student supervisors assumed an air of indignation at the poor turnout, claiming that the absentees were irresponsible and didn't appreciate the seriousness of the war. But in fact no one knew if the other students and teachers were alive or dead. Among the students and teachers who had come were some whose houses had burned down or whose family members were missing. On top of that, all our belongings had been incinerated in the weapons storehouse at the university, as I mentioned.

I found these comments quite offensive and wanted to say something to the student supervisors, but I held my tongue. I had dinner early, with some students who had just arrived, after which we went off to the room allotted to us. It was in quite a shambles. The window frames had been warped and dislodged by the blast and the floor was littered with glass fragments, as was the hallway outside.

The students and I sat down on the tatami floor. We hardly spoke to one another and no one volunteered to clean up. We felt uneasy and restless, as if we'd been thrown into a police detention cell and awaited interrogation. I wanted to listen to the news on the radio but the station had been destroyed, as had the newspaper offices. Trains were out of service too, and all this isolation only served to make us more nervous.

The dormitory had a desolate, deserted air about it because all the students who'd arrived earlier, apart from the supervisors, had split up into search parties and gone off to the various rescue stations to see if they could find anyone from the factory or university who had been wounded. As it happened, the factory had not been operating on the day of the bombing, because August 6 had been one of the "down days" on which no electricity was to be used, as an economy measure. So many of the factory workers and students had gone into the city for the day. Every now and then, there would be a commotion outside as wounded were brought in on stretchers and taken off to the dormitory sickroom.

—January 9, 1946

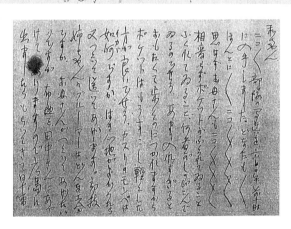

Letters, spring 1945, from the author (top) and his wife, Fumiyo (bottom). (Translations start on pages 176 and 181, respectively.)

Letter
7

Meeting
August 7–8, 1945

Fumiyo,

The letter I'm writing today is about happiness, even if that happiness was just the last burst of light that a candle gives before it goes out.

Later on the evening of August 7, a little past seven, I heard someone outside the dormitory calling my name. I hurried out and saw that it was Nakamura, a student who'd been staying at the dormitory for some time.

"Sir, Mrs. Ogura is at the Fuchu national school!"

"Eh? At Fuchu?"

At first I was astounded, rather than elated. I thought that he must be wrong. Fuchu is at least five or six kilometers from Funairi, so I couldn't imagine your having taken refuge there. What's more, it's to the east, while I had been looking for you in the west and southwest. But Nakamura soon convinced me.

He said that he had been looking at the injured in the gym of the Fuchu national school, to see if there were any workers from the factory or people from the university among them. Suddenly he heard you calling out, asking him how I was. You must have recognized his uniform as our university's, and thought that he might know something about me. Nakamura of course realized that you must be my wife. He wanted to get you out of there immediately, but there were no spare stretchers. So he made arrangements to have you brought to the sickroom of the factory dormitory as soon as a stretcher became available. After assuring you that I was safe at the dormitory, he'd hurried back here.

Nakamura was not a student of mine and I didn't know him at all until then. When I'd arrived at the dormitory office that day after my futile search for you and Kinji, Nakamura was heading out with some young factory workers; they were carrying stretchers and planned to bring back any fellow workers or university students who might have been injured and taken to the various rescue stations. We had briefly introduced ourselves at that time, so he knew that I was at the factory. That was probably the first time he'd seen or even heard of me. I often wonder what would have happened if Nakamura and I had not happened to meet in the office. This merest coincidence had restored the vital link between you and me. I'm sure that you would call it the work of the gods, but I was in no state to give any serious thought to things like that at the time.

Nakamura said there were other wounded people at the school in Fuchu who needed urgent attention, so it was decided that I would accompany the party that was to travel to Fuchu to fetch you. Four young factory workers were already waiting with a stretcher. It was growing dark when we set out through the back gate. I followed the others, who all walked in silence. They seemed familiar with the route. It was a gently sloping country road. From time to time, we saw people going the other way, with wounded victims on stretchers or in handcarts. They too walked along without speaking. Whenever someone passed, I smelled the faint odor of death that reminded me of the night before, when I'd looked for you and Kinji at the Koi national school.

The evening soon grew dark and moonless but I could still make out the outline of the road. Without realizing it, I had overtaken the others. I tried to slow down a bit but soon noticed I was well ahead of them again. My mind was a jumble of questions. Were you burned? Physically wounded? Where and how badly were you injured?

Soon we were at the gate of the school in Fuchu. A few people could be seen moving around in the light of a bonfire burning in the school yard. Sheets of paper posted on a blackboard near the bonfire fluttered, fanned by the flames. I gave your name to some people there, and said that we'd come to take you with us. A middle-aged woman standing near the blackboard scanned the lists. She pointed off to the left and said, "She's in that gym." Apparently the sheets of paper contained the names of the victims at the school.

I asked the young men to wait outside and went into the gym alone. I was assailed by the now-familiar pungent odor of death. In the dim light of a few candles, I could see several rows of "living corpses." However, there weren't as many as there had been at the Koi national school.

Some lay motionless, as if dead. Some were moving and others sitting up. It was probably just as well that I couldn't see the contorted agony on individual faces in the dim light. But it was also difficult for me to recognize anyone. So while taking care not to step on any of the victims, I bent over and peered into one face after another, starting from the door and working my way back. Yet I couldn't find you. I came to what I thought was the last of the victims and I still hadn't found you.

When I approached, some people closed their eyes indifferently while others simply ignored me. Sometimes a victim would stare back reproachfully, but with their eyes vacant; these stares tore at my heart. These poor people must have been peered and stared at time and again. They must also have been waiting, hoping that the next face to approach would be that of a beloved family member or friend. They had passed a day and a night this way, and now a second day was coming to a close. There were one or two rice balls placed beside each of these victims but I didn't see anyone eating.

I didn't want to, but since I still hadn't found you, I went through the rows again, this time from the inside toward the entrance. Still to no avail. In my third attempt, I went along the rows, calling your name in a low voice. I'd come to the end of the last row and was about to turn around, when I heard a soft murmur near my feet.

"She was here till just a while ago."

I looked down and saw a woman, her head bandaged, sitting on the floor with her legs stretched out in front of her. Her legs were injured too, and she cradled a baby in her arms. The space next to her was vacant and two rice balls were lying there on the corner of the straw mat. She raised her head as I stooped down toward her.

"You're from the university, aren't you?"

"Yes," I said.

"She was here till a little while ago," she repeated. On hearing that, I ran outside without even thinking to thank her. The young factory workers were sitting at the entrance, their legs extended in front of them and the stretcher propped up against the wall.

"Couldn't you find her?"

"No."

"She might be over there."

I looked in the direction where he was pointing. I could see a row of five or six bodies on the ground near the corner of the school yard, silhouetted by the flames of the bonfire. You can't be dead, I said, as I began walking toward the row of bodies. The individual forms became more distinct as I got closer.

There you were.

I couldn't see your face yet but I recognized you at once. I ran toward you. Even though it was dark, there were flies buzzing around. Your face, hands and legs were swathed in white bandages.

"Fumiyo, it's me! What happened?"

You didn't answer right away, though you must have recognized me in the light of the fire. I could see your eyes through the bandages; I could see your nose and your mouth. But your eyes looked like they had been stripped of emotion. You must have known, through Nakamura, that I was coming to get you, but you seemed to be utterly despondent.

You looked at me blankly and said very quietly, "'That was a huge lightning bolt,' I thought. Then I lost consciousness. This was in front of the Fukuya department store."

"In front of Fukuya's?"

The desolate scene I had seen the day before of all the corpses in front of the department store flashed through my mind.

"Anyway, let's get you on the stretcher."

The men had the stretcher ready and were standing by. I went around to hold up your head. One of the workers held your legs while another supported your hips. The three of us lifted you while the other two slid the stretcher under you.

The young men, apparently now accustomed to this sort of thing, lifted the stretcher effortlessly and started off. I walked alongside.

The minute I saw you, I thought you would eventually recover. Since the day before, I had become all too familiar with victims suffering terrible burns and injuries. You seemed to be burned only on the exposed parts of your body—your face, arms, legs. Your clothes were in tatters, but they had remained on your body. From what little I knew about burns, yours did not appear that serious. I was sure you would recover.

Over those four kilometers in the darkness of night, I matched my pace to that of the young men and listened to your intermittent account. You were in full possession of your senses. But the few words you spoke then would prove to be the last completely coherent speech you would ever make. So I want to set down the gist of what you told me, since it is the only record of your experiences.

You had left home intending to visit your sister Setsuko in Jigozen to discuss some evacuation arrangements. But when you came to the streetcar stop at Dobashi, you suddenly changed your mind and went to Hatchobori to buy a special frostbite ointment from a drugstore near Fukuya's which you had heard might be closing down, due to the worsening war situation. You thought you'd buy some of that ointment for Kazuko, who was chronically susceptible to frostbite in the winter. You'd gotten the ointment and were waiting at the streetcar stop for a car bound for Koi, thinking to transfer there to Jigozen, when the flash occurred.

You lost consciousness for a while after that, but it seems that this is what happened to you. You were thrown onto the hard pavement by the violent blast and knocked unconscious. You'd fallen on your back and bruised your shoulders and hips badly. (I didn't know about these injuries till I was cleansing your body, after you had passed away. You'd probably been unaware of them yourself.) As I said, you had also been burned on the exposed parts of your body. It's strange though that your burns were not so bad. Others who were in the same area at the time received burns far worse than yours, with their clothes all scorched and tattered. Maybe you were shielded from the flash by some buildings or people. Nearly everyone in the vicinity was killed on the spot. But it seems that a few victims regained consciousness and crawled out from among the corpses. This apparently happened to you too.

When you became conscious, you were standing at the east end of Kyobashi Bridge, wearing only one wooden *geta* clog. Your parasol and carryall were gone. Fires were breaking out everywhere and waves of people were surging toward Hiroshima Station. Soon you were caught up in the crowd, being propelled along.

You crossed Enko Bridge and the streetcar line and continued past the railroad crossing at Atagocho. From that point on, there were fewer people around, probably because many had moved off toward Nigitsu, Ozu, Danbara and other areas. You stopped walking then, not because of the pain but because you were so tired.

Fire had not yet spread to the area. An elderly woman standing in front of her shop suggested you rest a while. You took her advice and sat down just inside the entryway. At that point you were overcome with nausea, and vomited a little. The woman gave you some water, which made you feel a little better. So you got up and started walking again. But you had no idea where to go. The old lady had told you that you were in Atagocho. You remembered that the home of a former pupil of yours was located in the uptown section of Onagacho, not very far away.* So you vaguely thought that you would go there. While walking, however, you came to what looked like a school. It turned out to be the Matsumoto Commercial Middle School in Onagacho.

The people there applied some mercurochrome to your wounds and bandaged your face, arms and legs. While you were resting, you were told that fire was approaching the area, and that you should flee. You then headed for the hilly ground leading to Ochigodao, where you sank, utterly exhausted, to the ground and lay there. Some soldiers who were busy hauling supplies up and down the hills in that area told you that it was dangerous to lie there, and asked you to get off the road. But you no longer had the strength to stand up and walk. So you just slid down to the shoulder of the road. You were crouched there, your back hurting badly, when a truck came along and picked you up.

The truck was full of wounded people like yourself. You didn't know where they were taking you, but when the truck finally stopped you were at the Fuchu national school. It was evening by then, and you spent the night on the wooden floor of the school gym. People were dying around you and you wondered if you might not be next.

The next day people came looking for family members and relatives and took some victims away with them. You became despondent then because you had been taken off to a place where you had no relatives or connections, and you realized that there was little hope of anybody's coming to look for you. So when you had seen that student, caught his attention and learned that I

---

* [Fumiyo was a teacher of home economics until she began to have children.]

was safe at the dormitory, your eyes flooded with tears of joy. Later though, you found it difficult to stand the wait or bear the suffocating atmosphere of the gym. So you had crawled outside to the spot where I finally found you.

Walking alongside you, listening to your account, I was very worried about Kinji. I couldn't bring myself to ask you though, because I remembered all too well the deranged woman I'd seen the day before, whom I suspected had lost her child.

But no sooner had you finished telling me about your experiences than you asked, "I wonder what happened to Kin-chan?"

I felt like I had been hit on the head with a truncheon, but I merely asked you, in as unconcerned a tone as I could muster, "Why, where was he?"

"I didn't take him with me. My brother and his family were looking after him."

The matter-of-fact way in which you said that stunned me, even more than your initial question had.

"My God!" I wanted to shout, but I held my tongue. Controlling the turmoil inside me as best I could, I said that he must be all right, then, since Funairi hadn't burned.

"Is that so?" you said with an air of relief, and fell silent. I didn't say anything else, either. I couldn't.

Soon we were at the factory dormitory, and we put you into one of the sickrooms.

"Now that we're here, you can relax. Have a good rest. I need to go to the university now because I have something urgent to tell the people there." You'll remember that that's what I told you when I returned from a short visit to my room in the dormitory.

"Really?" you had replied in an unprotesting but forlorn tone.

"Don't worry. I've asked the students here to look after you. I'll be back by tomorrow morning," I said. You were quiet.

I went back to my room and asked the students to take care of you while I was away. I explained the situation to a colleague in the dormitory and then left immediately to look for Kinji. I don't know what came over me when I lied to you and dashed out like that. I had of course already been to your brother's house, which was burned to the ground, and I knew I had virtually no possibility of finding Kinji in the dark when I had failed to turn up any trace of him in broad daylight. But still, I felt compelled to try again.

Using a borrowed flashlight, I retraced my steps of the previous day and started walking toward Hiroshima. It was nearly midnight. Though there had been a fair amount of vehicular and pedestrian traffic during the day, the roads were practically empty now except for a few people I encountered coming from the city. I couldn't see their faces in the dark but I had the feeling that they'd been wandering around in the wreckage looking for missing relatives or friends till late in the night and were only now returning home, after a fruitless search. Two or three times, I came across people pulling handcarts loaded with what looked like lumps of flesh; I couldn't tell if the bodies inside were dead or alive.

Occasionally, I would see a figure on the roadside that looked close to death, and then the person would startle me by calling out.

"Is Kaitaichi near here?"

"Is this the way to Aki-nakano?"

They always asked directions, although they were not moving. Each time they spoke, I felt as if I was being addressed by the dead. These people had probably barely managed to drag themselves out of the ruins and were trying to reach the homes of family or friends.

"You're almost there!" I would say. "Go straight down this road."

As I approached the city, I could see flames flickering everywhere from residual embers.

When I entered the area which had been devastated, the same desolate scenery I had seen earlier greeted me and I wondered what I was doing there in that foul air again.

The road was very dark but I used the flashlight sparingly as I wanted to save the batteries for searching the vicinity of our now-nonexistent home.

I often stumbled when my feet would get tangled in downed power lines. Or I'd tread on something rubbery which, when I shone the flashlight on it, would turn out to be a corpse. Even though I became used to the dark, I felt it would be easier to go along the streetcar lines. So, after crossing Kyobashi Bridge, I walked toward the streetcar bridge that I had used the day before.

As I reached the area where our house had stood, I began to have grave doubts about what I could possibly accomplish by going there again.

Anyway, I stopped at the rescue station on the Eba streetcar line that I'd visited the day before. The "living corpses" were still laid out in rows. I switched on the light and looked carefully at each victim. But Kinji was not among them.

I decided against going back to the site of our house. There was nothing to be gained from it at this hour. Instead I started walking toward Koi, then changed my mind again and decided to go further on, to see your sister Setsuko in Jigozen. There was always a chance that your brother's family had gone there with Kinji.

It was a faint hope, but the only one I had.

I passed Koi quickly, with only the sound of my heels on the hard asphalt echoing in the night. Rice paddies stretched away on both sides of the road and the night air, free finally from the odor of death, was refreshing. From Kusatsu, the road runs along the coast and the soft rustling of the waves there was the first sound of nature I'd heard since the bombing. After a time I came to the place where the main street of Inokuchi runs parallel to the Miyajima Line.

Seeing the railroad brought to mind the most vivid recollection of Kinji's high-pitched voice calling out the names of stations, in order, as he played trains, one of his favorite games: "Next stop, Arate! Inokuchi! Jissen Jogakko!"

Suddenly I was terrified that this sharp image of him must mean that he was dead. I sat down weakly on the ground in front of the house I happened to be passing. I took out a cigarette and struck a match. I thought I sensed someone moving in the darkness beneath the eaves of the house, and then a figure sidled up to me.

"How far are you going?" he asked.

He appeared to be my age. He told me that his house in Kakocho had been destroyed. His wife, who was in the kitchen at the time, died in the raging fire that followed. Together with his aged father and four children, he had managed to struggle free from the debris and had fled to an acquaintance's home in Koi, where they had been staying since. It was still too early to recover his wife's remains, so he had decided to go to a relative's home in Miyauchimura for the time being. They had set out in the evening to avoid the worst heat of the day, but as his foot had been crushed and his aged father and young children had sustained various minor injuries, they had not made much progress. They had heard that train service had started up again, and that evacuees were being transported free of charge. So he said they were waiting till morning, when they could travel by train.

I offered him a cigarette, which he accepted and smoked with obvious relish. I thought that maybe I would wait for the train too, but when I saw that it was only four in the morning, I realized I could get to Jigozen on foot by the time the trains started running. So I said goodbye to the man and continued on my way. As daybreak approached, the stars in the summer sky looked truly beautiful.

I kept up a good pace; Itsukaichi and Hatsukaichi were now behind me. From time to time I heard a ghostly voice calling out the names of the stations.

It was light when I arrived at Setsuko's house. The front door was open. I dashed right in and called her name.

She came out from the kitchen. "My goodness!" Then, leaning into the next room, "Kin-chan, your daddy's here!"

"Kinji's here?"

"Yes. He came with my brother and his family. Where's Fumiyo?"

"I found her in Fuchu."

"Fuchu?"

"Yes. How is Kinji?"

Just then I saw him standing there, staring wide-eyed.

I rushed over and hugged him hard.

"Ow! That hurts!"

I relaxed my hold as he struggled. His abdomen was heavily bandaged and mercurochrome had been dabbed here and there on his face and limbs.

I started telling Setsuko how I'd found you, and your story of what you had endured. She then explained that when your brother and his family arrived with Kinji at her house on the afternoon of the sixth, they'd said that you'd left that morning, saying you were going off to visit Setsuko in Jigozen. She and your brother had looked for you on the seventh. They had searched all day in the western part of Hiroshima, from Dobashi to Koi, and had given up that night in despair.

Your brother Tetsuji's family was sleeping under a large mosquito net in the tatami-matted living room, but Tetsuji soon got up and came over to talk with us. He had been at the office at the time of the bombing and had escaped injury. Kinji was barely hurt at all, and on hearing that you were alive, he began to fret, saying he wanted to go see you.

I gave a brief account of how your brother Hideichi and your sister Aiko and their families were faring. Without going into the room where the others were sleeping, I went to the kitchen and had a quick breakfast. I then left, hoping to get a train and return to you as soon as possible, to let you know that I had found Kinji alive and well.

The two days and two nights of mental anguish suddenly seemed far in the past; I felt elated. I am a bit ashamed now of my lack of sympathy for others who had lost or were still looking for their loved ones. But I couldn't suppress my joy at the time.

—*January 25, 1946*

Letter
8

The Day of the Imperial Rescript
August 8, 1945

Fumiyo,

As you know, for the last four years, the government has referred to the eighth of every month as the "Day of the Imperial Rescript" in commemoration of December 8, 1941, when the imperial rescript was issued declaring war against the United States and the British Empire. The authorities did this to mark the outbreak of hostilities which they themselves started. They also urged all of us, women and children included, to go to Gokoku Shrine that day and pay homage to warriors who had fallen in past wars. They made citizens who did not have enough to eat take part in regular early morning fire drills, and freely interrupted the school day or the work being done in factories to hold ceremonies commemorating the declaration of war. As you know, anyone who didn't take part was considered at best ignorant and at worst unpatriotic.

Yet August 8, 1945 was a joyful day for me because the anxieties that had plagued me on the sixth and seventh had by then completely vanished. The eighth was the day that dawned once I learned that both you and Kinji were alive. From what I had seen in the two days I spent wandering the streets looking for you—or your corpses—I was hopeful that the war would now end. By the eighth, I was certain it would.

The weather was very good that day. I wanted to let you

know as soon as possible that Kinji was safe and well. I decided to go to Koi, the terminal station on the suburban Miyajima Line, which I'd heard had started running again. Then I would have to walk across the city, from west to east. The streetcar lines in the city had been completely destroyed and the government railroad between Kaitaichi and Itsukaichi had not operated since the bombing.

On the eighth, I came across several broken bridges. There had been no problem between Koi and Fukushimacho, but Fukushima Bridge had been destroyed. I walked further upstream and crossed the river at a particularly shallow spot. I walked on toward Honkawa Bridge, but it was down as well. So I had to go around, to Aioi Bridge, which I'd crossed the night before.

When crossing Aioi Bridge in the dark I hadn't noticed that all its parapets, except a few in the southeast corner, were gone, and that the walkways on either edge were just wobbling slabs of broken concrete. It looked as if they'd been blown up from below, but I couldn't really guess how the blast had struck. The telephone poles were all leaning over, but had not actually fallen. I thought this strange at the time, but I noticed later that many tall poles and chimneys were still standing. The blast came directly from above in this part of the city, and perhaps slender objects like these, whose tops presented a small area to it, were not blown over unless they had been structurally weak in the first place. This tendency became more apparent as one approached the site of the blast. The big *torii* gate of Gokoku Shrine was still standing amid the burned ruins, as if nothing had happened.

It was relatively easy to walk on the roads of the incinerated city center. Since the blast had occurred directly overhead there, buildings and other structures were crushed and burned where they stood, rather than being blasted sideways. The demolition of houses to create firebreaks along the main city roads also appeared to have contributed to the relative lack of debris. One newspaperman who entered the devastated city on August 7 had even naively reported that he was amazed at the speed with which the streets had been cleared!

The main building of Gokoku Shrine lay in ruins. I found it ironic that although this was the eighth, there were no crowds there to commemorate the Day of the Imperial Rescript. The scene there had been quite different a month earlier.

From there I went across the West Parade Ground. All the army facilities close to what had been Hiroshima Castle were now ashes. These included the army divisional headquarters, the military police headquarters, the main army hospital, the hospital annex, the army social club and the army uniform warehouse. I had expected to see a great deal of devastation, but I was dumbfounded to see that the area had been completely obliterated.

I realized now why I had seen so few soldiers in the city after the bombing. Normally they would be the first to be called out to help in an emergency. Obviously a lot of military, and particularly army, personnel had died in the blast.

I already knew that the main tower of the castle was gone, because I hadn't seen it from Hakushima the day before, but now I saw that the entire castle had disappeared without a trace. Not even the turrets or front gate survived. Only the moat and the stone foundation remained, presenting a pathetic sight.

Looking down into the moat, I saw numerous dead fish floating in the water, mouths open. They looked as if they had been dynamited. Which they practically had, being this close to the center of the explosion, I thought. The goldfish in the water cistern in front of our house had survived, I supposed, because Funairi was some distance from the site of the blast.

I walked across the area where the temporary Diet building had stood during the Sino-Japanese War and came to Hatchobori. I didn't notice whether the pine tree planted to mark the spot of the emperor's rest house was still standing. It had probably been obliterated too. The obelisk commemorating the 1900 Boxer Rebellion looked very dilapidated.

When I came to the street, I noticed pieces of paper pasted on the burned remains of buildings and electric power poles. They were all proclamation notices signed jointly by the "Hiroshima

Security Commander" and "Commander of the Army Marine Corps." I can't remember now what was written on them, but what caught my eye was the two signatures. Everyone knew of the Army Marine Corps Commander because his name was associated with the army's water-borne Akatsuki Corps, but I had not heard the title "Hiroshima Security Commander" before. I looked carefully at the notices again to see if they were not signed by the "Martial Law Commander," but they definitely read "Hiroshima Security Commander." At the time, we all knew that the Second Army, the Chugoku Military District, the Fifth Division and the military police were all based in Hiroshima. Yet the proclamations included the signature of the "Hiroshima Security Commander," not any of the other commanders.

The army in Hiroshima must have been annihilated, I thought. Even to a layman like me, these proclamations clearly indicated that only the commander of the Akatsuki Corps had survived. All the others were dead.

I was now firmly convinced that the war was coming to an end.

I became anxious to hear the latest news. I walked as fast as I could back to the factory dormitory, where I was sure newspapers would now have arrived, and where I could also listen to the radio. However, somewhere along the way, I managed to take a wrong road. I'd meant to take a shortcut to the factory, and should have been heading in the direction of Aiko's house. But I found myself in front of Hiroshima Station, which was not really surprising, considering that all the landmarks had been obliterated.

Since I was at the station, I went in, thinking to walk on the railroad track. The wreckage of the main building was the only thing standing, as I mentioned. A lot of people were walking in either direction, as if the tracks were sidewalks. I simply joined the stream of people and began walking.

It was well after noon when I returned to the factory dormitory. I had gone on foot to Jigozen and back, a total distance of over forty kilometers, since leaving you the night before. Later I was amazed at the distance I'd walked. I noticed a faint smell of corpses in the corridor. As I entered the dormitory's sickroom, I was relieved to see you were sleeping soundly.

When you awoke, your eyes still had that vacant look. You gazed at me but didn't say anything. When I told you that Kinji and your brother and his family were safe and well, all you said was, "Is that so?" I felt your forehead and your underarm, but you didn't seem to have a fever, so I just assumed that you were completely exhausted. Sitting beside your bed, I ate the packed lunch Setsuko had given me. Then I went over to the dormitory building, where I did see a newspaper for the first time since the bombing; it had been brought in by a student who'd arrived that day from Kobe. It reported the news about Hiroshima in the form of an "announcement" by the imperial headquarters. This announcement referred to a new type of bomb, describing it in that institution's inimitable prose style—at first seemingly comprehensible, but on closer inspection, quite unintelligible.

That day, a perfunctory welcoming ceremony was the only thing scheduled at the dormitory for the morning; no actual work was required. We had all finally been allocated rooms, and I went off to lie down. As I hadn't slept at all the night before and had been walking around continuously for two days, I was exhausted. Also, now that I'd found you and Kinji, my worries were over for the moment. I closed my eyes and felt my body being drawn straight down into an abyss.

But I couldn't fall asleep; my nerves were still on edge. I couldn't help but smile wryly as I thought of the announcements from the imperial headquarters. By then, I was accustomed to such hackneyed expressions as "considerable damage" and "details are being investigated." But given what I had seen and heard over the past three days, the use of these phrases to describe the effect of the explosion showed the degree of confusion and panic that gripped the military establishment. Damage incurred by a local city had, to my knowledge, never before been the subject of an imperial headquarters announcement. My mind raced with images of the devastation I'd seen and absurd visions of the officers in the imperial headquarters trying to convince people that this new bomb was nothing to be afraid of.

The war is definitely coming to an end, I thought again as I lay looking up at the ceiling.

If at that time I had known about President Truman's radio address of August 6, I probably would have been angry as well as cynical. Military censorship prevented us from learning about Truman's statement on the sixth until August 15, the day the imperial rescript announcing the surrender was issued. As you were a victim of the bombing, let me now repeat a few passages of Truman's address:

"Sixteen hours ago an American airplane dropped one bomb on Hiroshima, an important Japanese Army base. That bomb had more power than 20,000 tons of T.N.T. It had more than two thousand times the blast power of the British "Grand Slam" which is the largest bomb ever yet used in the history of warfare … We are now in a position to promptly and completely destroy all production facilities possessed by Japan."*

This was followed by a description of the tremendous efforts made by America in the research and development of the atomic bomb, as well as a statement of U.S. readiness to "obliterate more rapidly and completely every productive enterprise the Japanese have above ground in any city."

Near the end of his speech Truman said, "It was to spare the Japanese people from utter destruction that the ultimatum of July 26 was issued at Potsdam. The fact that we can release atomic energy ushers in a new era in man's understanding of nature's forces. Atomic energy may in the future supplement the power that now comes from coal, oil and falling water."

---

* ["Statement by the President Announcing the Use of the A–Bomb at Hiroshima" (August 6, 1945). In "Public Papers of the Presidents of the United States: Harry S. Truman (Containing the Public Messages, Speeches, and Statements of the President April 12 to December 31, 1945)." Washington: United States Government Printing Office, 1961.]

But I've digressed. Let me tell you more about the things I saw that day. I felt that there were now, three days after the bombing, many more people moving around in the wreckage. These included many who had come from outside the city to help with rescue operations, people who had been in Hiroshima at the time but had escaped injury or were only slightly hurt as well as some soldiers, although as I mentioned their number was fewer than one would have expected. All these people were involved in distributing relief supplies to victims, clearing roads, retrieving corpses and so on.

Placards noting the location of temporary "offices" of the various town assemblies and neighborhood associations were posted up in a range of places. Thanks to the efforts of all these people, there were now fewer corpses lying on the roads. But the weather had been hot and clear for three days, and the stench of rotting flesh was stronger than ever. Places where heaps of maggot-ridden corpses swarmed with flies were especially unbearable.

Obviously, corpses could not just be gathered together and left in the street. So they were being cremated in any open spaces available in the burned-out city. At national schools, hospitals and rescue stations, unclaimed corpses were disposed of in this manner. Some were identified by family members who then took over the cremations, but most were unceremoniously incinerated. There was probably no other way to deal with all the bodies. In some places, I believe the bodies were buried right there because they couldn't all be cremated.

I forget where it was, but at one crossroads somebody had erected a simple booth, using odd lumber and boards from nearby ruins. It reminded me of the stalls set up by the peddlers who sell potted plants at shrines on festival days. On the shelves were rows of small packets made from old folded newspaper, again like the ones in which peddlers wrap seeds. However, each of these packages contained a small quantity of ash and had a name and address written on them. Many didn't even have names—only a description, such as "Male about thirty years old" or "Forty-year-old female." There were some bereaved families, including a number of my acquaintance, who claimed such ashes solely on the basis of the packet's description of the victim and the location of the body.

Smoke from the wreckage had died down considerably and had now been replaced by smoke from cremations. The burned-out area had literally become one vast crematorium. Meanwhile people had begun to retrieve the bleached bones of loved ones who'd been trapped and incinerated under crushed houses. I saw people lay two charred corpses side by side, trying to identify which was which. This kind of thing went on for days afterwards.

In general, people who found those they were looking for— even if in the form of "living corpses" or charred remains—could be considered fortunate. I saw a great many dispirited people going from one rescue station to the next, looking in vain for a sign of missing family members. Many visited all the rescue stations, including those in the suburbs and on neighboring islands, to no avail. They were to continue their futile search for weeks, months or longer. There were lots of victims who survived the bombing but subsequently succumbed to their injuries, without ever being found by their families.

Many who had taken refuge in the homes of friends and acquaintances in or near the city now moved further afield. This was partly due to the impending expiration of the certificates entitling evacuees to free travel on government railroads. This exodus from the city became more pronounced after August 9, when services on the Sanyo Line were fully restored. Without exception, evacuees wore clothes that were scorched and tattered; many also nursed some kind of injury. They usually had no personal belongings, perhaps apart from a package containing the ashes of a deceased relative. They presented an awesome, rather than a pitiful, sight.

When their houses collapsed and caught fire, survivors who were at home at the time of the bombing lost their emergency supply kits and the satchels into which they had carefully placed wallets, purses, bankbooks, bonds, certificates for securities and other documents. Those who were outside at the time had practically everything they were carrying with them wrenched away by the force of the blast. Therefore, many survivors had literally nothing to their names. In this respect their plight was more terrible than that of survivors of conventional air raids in other cities. Our family was in just this predicament because all documentary proof of what little we owned was in the bag snatched from your hand by the blast.

The events of August proved to be quite confusing. People who had been living on the outskirts of Hiroshima and whose houses were not damaged were now hurriedly leaving for the countryside because of rumors that those areas would be the next bomb's targets. So some who had lost their homes in the city were able to rent quite solid houses in the suburbs after only one night's search. But then, following the emperor's announcement of the surrender on August 15, the original owners—their safety now assured—promptly headed back to the city, creating new problems.

To complicate things further, at the tail end of the war, when the army hurriedly started building temporary barracks on the hills around Ushida, rumors circulated that the military was fortifying the area for a major battle. You can imagine the fear among the evacuees who had recently settled there.

While the turmoil that gripped the population was understandable under the circumstances, the inefficiency and bullheadedness that prevailed at the imperial headquarters at the time—which only gradually came to light after the surrender—was astounding. The derision I had begun to feel for the people there seems to have been well grounded.

—April 13, 1946

Kazuko (first row, on left, with white patch on shirt) and her classmates at the temple, spring 1945. The broad smiles seen here are characteristic of all the group photographs taken by teachers for mailing to parents back in Hiroshima. Compare this photo with the one on page 48, taken by one of the girls' parents.

Hypocenter

August 9–10, 1945

Fumiyo,

You were in the sickroom of the factory dormitory from the night of August 7 through the evening of the tenth. I'm afraid I didn't take much care of you during that time, but only stayed at your bedside for a short time during the mornings and evenings.

You may have felt neglected and thought me heartless. More likely you told yourself that it was for the sake of the country. In any case, you slept a great deal, and never complained. You didn't say anything about the food or the medical care you were receiving. I mistakenly assumed that this was because your injuries were relatively minor. I admit that I didn't give it much thought beyond that. After all, I was busy supervising the students at the factory and I was the only instructor there at the time.

One thing I never managed to tell you when you were with me was that I had gone around to Honshoji Temple, where the ashes of our dear departed Toshiko were kept.* The temple had burned to the ground. There was a notice posted up in the ruins saying that the old head priest, whom you knew so well, had died. I looked everywhere in the area where the ash repository had been for the urn containing Toshiko's ashes, but it was nowhere to be seen. So I just scooped up a handful of ordinary ash

---

* [The author and his wife had a fourth child, Toshiko, who was born on September 1, 1944 and died of the measles on February 17, 1945.]

from the vicinity, wrapped it in a piece of paper and brought it back with me. As when I lied to you on the night of the seventh and said I was going to the university but actually went to look for Kinji, I didn't tell you about my visit to the temple because I didn't want to upset you.

On the ninth and tenth, I went with the students to the university to help clean up the debris. The situation in the city was not much different from what it was on the eighth, although there were now more people cleaning up and doing relief work, as well as more people looking for relatives and retrieving bodies. Columns of smoke from cremations done in the open air spiraled in the air, and there were fewer bodies left now on the streets.

When I got to the university, I was shocked by what I learned about the extent of the devastation.

Human bones were found among the wreckage of equipment and the ashes of books and documents in our laboratory. Fortunately, it appears that nobody was in my classroom at the time of the blast. An ancient Yayoi pottery specimen lay miraculously unbroken on the floor.

Though it was generally possible to guess the identity of skeletons found inside the rooms, it was impossible to do so with those found in the corridors. The total number of fatalities, including those who died subsequently, was more than 130. These consisted mainly of teachers and some students from the science departments as well as members of the clerical staff, since teachers and students, like us, from the liberal arts departments had been sent to assist at factories and were not on campus at the time.

Professor Watanabe told me that windowpanes shattered, walls caved in and people, desks, chairs and other objects were dashed against the walls the moment the blast occurred. Most of the victims were injured this way and some died instantly, with their skulls split open and their brains spilling out. The survivors, nearly all of whom were wounded, fled in all directions. These included the twenty teachers whose turn it had been to stay overnight at the university and the sixty student members of the university security unit. Therefore no one was present to put out the fires that broke out later. I'm told that the situation was the same on the third floor, in the offices of the Chugoku district governor.

This behavior may at first sound irresponsible, but actually you can't blame those concerned because they were no doubt thinking in terms of conventional bombs and incendiaries. No one could have understood at the time that a single bomb had caused such destruction in an instant. Even if a handful of injured personnel had stayed at their posts, it would have been futile. Even the most hardened military personnel, who exemplify the "military spirit" and are lauded as the "emperor's honorable shields," were at a complete loss as to how to respond in this situation.

As you know, the authorities were urging everyone to adopt the "military spirit" and emulate soldiers in all aspects of daily life. But one atomic bomb turned gallant soldiers into ordinary human beings in the twinkling of an eye. No "military spirit" was strong enough to stand up against the overwhelming power of the atomic bomb. But the use of this great a show of force was necessary to bring proponents of the "military spirit" to their senses. The catastrophe was brought on in part by the blind submission of loyal citizens to the exhortations of the proponents of this spirit. When you think of it in this way, it's hard to point fingers at anyone. I suppose the military, the government and ordinary citizens were all equally responsible.

Professor Watanabe's office was in the path of the blast but, by pure chance, a big partition screen that came flying toward him formed a protective barrier that prevented him from being seriously injured. It was a miracle that he escaped with only minor abrasions.

He also told me that the jacket he'd left hanging on the partition screen was blown out of the window. He found it later, caught on a broken window frame two rooms down. One expert explained that in an explosion there is a strong positive blast lasting for a fraction of a second, followed by an even shorter blast of negative pressure. Depending on the layout of buildings in the area, this alternation of positive and negative air pressure can cause a whirlwind effect. What happened to Professor Watanabe's jacket is a good illustration of this phenomenon, which has also been corroborated by others' experiences. Even a layman like me can understand the phenomenon a little.

The situation at other severely damaged schools and institutions seems to have been quite similar to that at the university.

Most institutions of higher learning in the city were so badly damaged that they were unfit for use. The only ones that were spared were the Prefectural Girls' College—your alma mater—and the Hiroshima teachers' training school. Nearly all the teachers and students of these schools had been mobilized for work in factories elsewhere, so there weren't very many casualties among them.

The middle schools were hard hit, with the buildings of many completely destroyed. They also suffered a high toll of casualties among the younger students, who were helping to create firebreaks, and their teachers. More than 7,000 students and teachers from Hiroshima middle schools died; about 2,500 were badly wounded.

I don't know the exact date I went there, but I remember it was drizzling as I walked through the ruins of the Prefectural First Girls' High School, which you attended before college. An expanse of broken roof tiles lay where the school had been. The ferroconcrete alumni hall stood in ruins in the southwest corner of the school yard, as did the lecture hall in the southeast corner; the steel frameworks of both were crushed. Quite by chance, I met a woman who I understand taught you in high school and also at the girls' college. We didn't talk long because of the rain, but I told her about you and she briefly recounted what happened at the school.

There was a short lecture that day for girls aspiring to become nurses, as well as an occupational training class for war widows. The teachers and students attending those events were all killed.

Students who were not feeling well and so were not able to go into the city on work assignments had just been dismissed when the blast occurred. Some managed to scramble into air-raid shelters and were unhurt, but many who were out in the school yard were badly burned. All the first-grade pupils died at Dobashi while helping to clear firebreaks. I was told that your former classmate and good friend who'd become a teacher at the school—I can't recall her name—lost her entire family at her home in Otemachi and that she herself died at the school. She had just returned from accompanying a group of students to do voluntary work in Kure. I understand that seventeen members of the teaching staff, including the principal, lost their lives, although I forgot to ask how many students were killed. I believe that this was comparable to the situation at other middle schools.

There were about thirty-five national schools in Hiroshima at the time. Of these, only about fifteen, located in the outskirts of the city, escaped being burned. The remaining twenty or so were completely destroyed. The national school associated with the university, which our children attended, was destroyed, as was the Fukuromachi primary school, where your brothers and sisters had gone.

I remember late last April when you and I saw Kazuko and Keiichi off at Hiroshima Station as they left for the countryside with their classmates. It didn't seem like a very reliable safety measure at the time, did it? As a matter of fact though, this precaution saved many lives. Many of these children were orphaned and made homeless in an instant, so our children were among the more fortunate.

A great many public servants were killed immediately, as government offices were clustered near the site of the explosion.

I learned later that one of the rare exceptions was the East Police Station, which escaped both serious damage and heavy casualties. I happened to pass by this police station on the sixth, seventh and eighth, and on each occasion officers were busily giving first aid and handing out emergency food supplies.

I've been using the phrase "center of the explosion" because it's familiar to you, but in fact we've begun using the new term "hypocenter" for this. Like "atomic bomb," it's now very well known.

On August 9, Dr. Yoshio Nishina, who is apparently Japan's leading nuclear physicist, was flown in by the army. He began conducting field surveys the next day and found that the new weapon was an "atomic bomb" and that the center of the explosion, or "hypocenter," was about two hundred meters south of the *torii* gate of Gokoku Shrine, at an altitude of about six hundred meters. On the ground, that would be roughly between the Central Post Office and the clinic on the north side which our good friend, Kiyoshi, had owned.

The explosion was accompanied by a blinding flash of light and intense thermal rays, followed by a tremendous blast of air. It is said that uranium 235 was used in the bomb dropped on Hiroshima and that the energy released came from splitting the uranium atom. I believe that ten million kilocalories of heat are produced from one gram of uranium 235. Therefore, ten billion kilocalories of energy can be obtained from a single kilogram. Experts think that one kilogram of uranium was used in the bomb dropped on Hiroshima, together with one ton of water. At the moment of the explosion, the water was subjected to temperatures of several tens of thousands of degrees centigrade. The vapor this produced formed a fireball twenty to thirty meters in diameter, which emitted tremendous amounts of radiation in the form of gamma rays, neutrons and so on.

The burns so many people suffered were thermal burns caused by the intensive heat rays. The illness brought on by radioactivity is called "radiation sickness." Although I first thought that you had sustained only minor burns, I learned later that you were actually suffering from this disease.

The "pageant of clouds and lights" that I saw that morning began when the fireball surged upward, assuming first a cylindrical and then a mushroom shape, with a cloud column boiling up from the ground level and spreading out sideways at the top. The fireball ascended to an altitude of about twelve thousand meters. I'm told that the reason why the fireball gave off numerous lightning-like flashes of light was that the wavelength of light grows shorter as the temperature of the light source increases. The temperature of the sun itself is only about six thousand degrees centigrade, so the heat of the radiation generated in this explosion is beyond all imagination.

Experts believe that the flash of light occurred with the initial explosion, which involved a huge amount of explosives, mainly magnesium, and took place at an altitude of about fifteen hundred meters. This triggered the fission of uranium 235, which was the main constituent of the bomb, setting off a chain reaction, with the final massive explosion occurring about six hundred meters above ground, as I mentioned.

The true nature of the bomb is being kept strictly confidential even in America, and so the investigations now being done by scientists in other countries are nothing more than conjecture and assumption. I am no scientist, but these are some of the things I saw and heard after the bombing.

A lot of attention lately has been focused on the hypocenter. Several times now I have walked past the Fukuya department store, which is of course where you were at the time of the bombing, and around the vicinity of the hypocenter. The difference between the ruins of Hiroshima and those of cities subjected to conventional bombing was clearly visible in the degree of destruction and fire damage found there. The obliteration of the Central Post Office and Sairenji Temple was understandable since these were made of wood, but Kiyoshi's clinic was a concrete building and still it was destroyed. I have little doubt that Kiyoshi and his family were killed. I have made inquiries about them but have not been able to learn anything. In the atomic bombing, many small concrete buildings were leveled. Even fairly large concrete buildings were severely damaged if they had any structural weakness.

I had always considered the Mitsui Bank building downtown

to be Hiroshima's finest building. The bank's name had changed, of course, when the government forced it to amalgamate with others into the "Imperial Bank" toward the end of the war. The building was now in ruins, with its roof collapsed and the entire structure leaning to one side. It had been a splendid-looking building, but its construction must have been defective.

Scenes of complete destruction were not limited to the hypocenter of course, but some of the more vivid examples were present there. For instance, roof tiles melted and fused together there like raw clay with the extreme heat. The surface of some tiles melted in streaks, with bead-like lumps forming as the tiles cooled. These phenomena could only be found near the hypocenter, and were not even common there. People must have collected tiles like that as souvenirs because there aren't many around now.

Whenever I have a chance, I go over that way and walk through the area of the hypocenter. In fact, I was there just the other day.

The sight of the Industry Promotion Hall, next to the hypocenter, never fails to move me. That old brick building, with its rather exotic dome, was well known in Hiroshima. Though the building was virtually destroyed, roof and floors both having caved in, the steel frame of the dome and the outer walls of the building are still standing. If you step over the rubble and into the remains of the building, you can look up and see the blue sky through the skeleton of the dome, making you feel as if you might be standing amid the ruins of Pompei.

The Motoyasu River flows immediately in front of it, with the northern, pointed end of the Jisenjibana delta located across the river. There wasn't a single house left standing on the delta. At full tide now you can see unobstructed reflections glimmering on the other side of the delta. In the old days, when there was a bridge there, you could easily cross straight over. Before the war, this was replaced with the T-shaped Aioi Bridge further upstream, and now you have to go north to the street where the streetcars run, turn left and go over the bridge. About midway across it, you turn left again and go down the stem part of the "T" to get to the delta. I usually follow this route when I'm in the vicinity. A large, rather forlorn-looking wooden column was erected recently in the delta area where Jisenji Temple stood, as a cenotaph for victims of the bombing.

I believe that the city authorities are planning to turn the area into a memorial park in the future and to build a commemorative hall and a peace monument there, but I personally think it would serve the purpose better to leave it all as it is.

After visiting this area, I usually cross Motoyasu Bridge further downstream and walk toward the hypocenter again. Motoyasu Bridge itself escaped destruction but it is said that dead soldiers were found lying neatly on the bridge in drill formation, in rows of four. I don't know if this is true or not.

That's what I typically do when I walk around the vicinity of the hypocenter. Then I catch a streetcar at the Aioi Bridge stop and go either to the university or to the lonely storehouse, carpeted with coarse straw mats, where I'm presently living.

The newspaper of August 17, 1945, reported that when George Bernard Shaw of England heard of Japan's unconditional surrender, he remarked that the war ended the moment the first atomic bomb was dropped but that the question of whether we have the right ever to use this weapon again remains highly problematical. The first part of his comment coincides with what I first thought soon after I saw the effects of the bomb. I am now pondering the question raised in the latter part of his remark. I felt a strange affinity for this great man of letters, and his skepticism, when I read this news item.

We have no one but ourselves to blame for the fact that we allowed our military leaders to stay in power and that we submitted to their authority. We have to accept the dropping of the bomb in expiation of these sins. In any case, that is my own view. Mankind, and the Japanese in particular, must strive to become wiser and more prudent in the future, so that the question of the right or need to use nuclear weapons will not arise.

Soon after the Allied occupation forces landed in Japan, approximately thirty foreign war correspondents visited Hiroshima to investigate the effects of the bombing. The correspondents apparently reported that Hiroshima was a place where only vultures could survive and that they would not have come, had they known the extent of the devastation they would confront here. A number of shacks have begun to spring up more recently, but right after the bombing it was indeed fit only for vultures.

The correspondents said that they had previously witnessed horrible destruction on many battlefronts but that they'd never seen anything like what happened in Hiroshima. I've never been to war, so I don't know firsthand how bad "horrible destruction" is, or where the "battlefronts" they referred to are. I assume that they were speaking of European battlegrounds and war-ravaged cities. Their words confirmed my own impression that the destruction visited on Hiroshima by the atomic bomb was the greatest of its kind that man had ever experienced.

I realize that I have not yet said much about the fate of the army in Hiroshima, a city that was known as a "military center." Two of your brothers and your brother-in-law were called up and they endured many years of hardship in the army. Only Tetsuji was able to be here at the time of your death. Your younger brother, Yokichi, with whom you were quite close, and Setsuko's husband, Benji Katsutani, your favorite of all your in-laws, were both demobilized later, though Yokichi had lost a leg.

Your brothers and some of their friends told me all kinds of stories about how the army fared in the bombing. They were able to speak freely at that point, since the restrictions on discussion of military matters had been lifted. You recall the stories they'd tell each time they came back from one of their many tours of duty following the Manchurian Incident. I'll tell you soon what your brothers and other people told me about the bombing's effect on the army.

—*May 10, 1946*

Letter

10

A Target for the Atomic Bomb

August 10–17, 1945

Fumiyo,

When I returned to the factory dormitory in the afternoon of the tenth, you begged me like a child to take you to Jigozen to see Kinji.

I had presumed the war would be over soon, and had thought to have you stay at the dormitory until it ended. But the Sanyo railroad had started running the day before and since Professor Shirai, one of the other supervisors, had finally arrived, I decided to leave matters at the dormitory to him and take you to Jigozen. Professor Shirai had not been at home at the time of the bombing and was not injured, but his house had collapsed and burned and his wife and son were missing. Still, he felt great responsibility for the work assigned him at the factory.

You'll remember that we left that evening, with me carrying you on my back. Stopping to rest every now and then, we made our way to the Kaitaichi railroad station. I didn't know until you showed it to me that you had a certificate indicating that you were a victim of the bombing. You said it was given to you at the rescue station. I'd gotten one too, at a temporary booth of the city office in front of Hiroshima Station. Using these certificates, we were able to take the train without paying any fares. To my dismay, however, the train stopped at Hiroshima Station and would go no further. So you will recall I brought you out of the

carriage and put you down on the platform. I had to leave you
lying there on the cold platform till well into the night. It was
pitch dark; not even a single candle was burning. I couldn't tell
for certain, but all the platforms seemed to be crowded with dis-
placed people like us.

You wanted some water so I went off to see if I could find any,
but I had a small accident. I fell down into a staircase on the platform that had lost its surrounding guardrails, and sprained my
right ankle and left wrist. It was very painful but I didn't say anything to you about it. We boarded a train that finally came in
around midnight and eventually arrived at Miyajimaguchi
Station, where we lay down together on the concrete platform
until dawn. We got on the first train that left on the morning of
August 11 and somehow managed to make our way to your sister's. You might have noticed that I was not very attentive to you
after we boarded the train at Hiroshima Station but in the dark
you couldn't see how I was wincing with pain from the fall I had
taken. I was actually having great difficulty when I was moving
you around or carrying you on my back. If it had been in the
daytime, we would have presented quite a pathetic sight. At least
the darkness spared us this humiliation. After asking Setsuko to
look after you, I immediately returned to the factory. Forgive me.
In light of my own experience over the previous few days, I felt
that I had to go back to the factory and take over so that Professor
Shirai could go out and search for his wife and child. You know
that I'm not so conscientious that I would leave my injured wife
or ignore my own injuries simply to get back to an assigned task.

From the eleventh, I was at the factory every day. The number
of students under my charge varied, but generally averaged only
about ten. Professor Mikio Yamamoto, who'd been stationed at
the factory for so long that he had come to be regarded as something like a senior member of the factory staff, was in charge of all
the students who had come there on work assignments.

University students staying at the dormitory served as student
supervisors of the middle-school-age boys and girls from middle

schools assigned to day labor at the factory; it was some of these supervisors who had said that people who didn't show up right after the bombing were unpatriotic.

Since the students in my charge were completely new to this work, they were assigned at first to train alongside the more experienced middle school pupils. They fashioned molds out of sand and poured molten iron into them to make the outer casings of hand grenades. I believe that seventy or eighty percent of the casings that they made failed to pass inspection, and had to be melted down and redone. As for me, I had my left arm in a homemade sling and needed to lean on a stick whenever I stood, because of my sprained right ankle, so about all I could do was watch and listen as the students toiled away.

After spending the entire day of the eleventh in this manner, I returned to the dormitory in the evening and saw a newspaper there for the first time in several days. Newspaper delivery started up again at about that time. The first item to catch my eye was a headline saying that the Soviet Union had declared war on Japan on the morning of August 9, and had invaded Manchuria. As was usually the case, it was reported that "our troops were fighting back bravely," but it was clear that the Japanese army was on the defensive and that it was fighting a losing battle. The day before, a colleague at the university had told me that a newspaper reporter from Osaka said that the Japanese government seemed to have commenced peace negotiations with the United States through the Soviet Union. I'd commented at the time that perhaps the Soviets wasn't as guileless as the Japanese government tended to believe. So when I read about the Soviet declaration of war on Japan and invasion of Manchuria, I wasn't too surprised; I had suspected that something like that might well happen. In any case, I was quite frankly more interested in stories about the bombing. Another headline on the same page startled me. It said, "New Type of Bomb Dropped on Nagasaki." It was in the form of an announcement issued by the Western District Military Command Center at 14:45 on August 9. It ended typically by saying that

"details are under investigation but damage has been extremely
light." What on earth were they trying to say, I wondered. Was it
because Nagasaki was smaller than Hiroshima that the destruction
there was regarded as "light"?

Professor Shirai stayed that night at the faculty room that had
been established at the dormitory. Anxiety and exhaustion
seemed to have taken their toll on the elderly gentleman. He was
normally quite easygoing, but had suddenly become withdrawn
and quiet. I too said practically nothing; I couldn't find the words
to console him. When I got into bed, I couldn't sleep because my
sprained wrist and ankle were throbbing with pain.

On the twelfth, Professor Shirai went out again to look for his
wife and child. I went to the factory alone and came back to the
dormitory alone that night. The newspaper headlines, spread over
five columns, shouted, "Grave threat to the continuance of the
imperial system and our very nation—but we shall fight our way
out of this. Together, a hundred million people can overcome
anything!" There were also messages to all military officers and
personnel issued by War Minister Anami and a message to the
nation from Information Bureau President Shimomura.

All were couched in the usual high-flown and nebulous language peculiar to such authorities, yet their desperation was
plainly evident between the lines.

I slipped into despondency. Although it was still light out, I
crawled into bed, very depressed. I closed my eyes, but couldn't
fall asleep because thoughts of you and Kinji kept crowding into
my mind. That day I had just received a letter from Kazuko and
Keiichi, which said that they went out every day to gather wild
vegetables and edible grasses to eat, so I was worried about them
too. My wrist and ankle also started hurting.

I picked up the newspaper again and began reading in bed. In
small print, the newspaper carried the text of President Truman's
statement aired on the radio at ten p.m. on August 9, which must
have been broadcast to coincide with the bombing of Nagasaki. I
thought that this was his first warning to Japan, because I didn't

know then that he had also broadcast a message immediately after Hiroshima was bombed.

"The world will note that the first atomic bomb was dropped on Hiroshima, a military base ... But that attack is only a warning of things to come. If Japan does not surrender, bombs will have to be dropped on her war industries and, unfortunately, thousands of civilian lives will be lost."[*]

Having seen for myself the force of this new bomb, I couldn't help thinking that this message was a frank and honest warning. The leaders of Japan's central government should come and see for themselves the destruction inflicted on Hiroshima, I thought.

The next column carried the detailed text of a message sent by the Japanese government on the tenth to the government of the United States, via the International Red Cross in Switzerland, protesting the use of the new bomb. I thought this was a completely useless gesture, and that such bravado in the face of a hopeless situation was a form of stupidity.

My mood was turning foul when I looked out the window and saw a crescent moon in the western sky. My thoughts turned back to you and Kinji.

Professor Shirai did not return to the dormitory that night, but did come back the next night, the thirteenth. He had found his wife and son at separate rescue stations. He was immensely relieved. Although both had been badly injured, their lives were not in danger.

The newspaper that same day had carried a story with the headline, "No Reason to Fear New-Style Bomb," and went on to review the so-called "countermeasures" against the atomic bomb that had first been made public on August 11.

Then came the fifteenth of August. As you know, I was back with

---

[*] ["Radio Report to the American People on the Potsdam Conference" (August 9, 1945). In "Public Papers of the Presidents of the United States: Harry S. Truman (Containing the Public Messages, Speeches, and Statements of the President April 12 to December 31, 1945)." Washington: United States Government Printing Office, 1961.]

you at Setsuko's house in Jigozen because it was one of the regular electric power "holidays" at the factory. We were told that an "important announcement" would be broadcast at noon. The emperor's message to the people was barely audible, due to poor reception, but we were able to gather, from the mention of an "official cabinet decree" and the explanation of the "process of negotiation" that was to follow, that Japan had accepted the terms of the Potsdam Declaration. Setsuko, sitting beside me, asked, "What does all this mean, anyway?"

"It means we have surrendered," I told her.

"Eh?" she exclaimed, with an air of incredulity.

I didn't feel sad, or bitter, or glad. I was a bit disheartened, I suppose, and quite relieved. I went to your bedside and said, "Japan has surrendered at last."

You opened your blank eyes wide and were silent for a while. Then your eyes brimmed with tears as you murmured, "I feel sorry for the emperor."

But your expression seemed to brighten a little when I said, "Now I'll be able to come and take good care of you."

I had to go back to the factory first though.

Almost all the students assigned to work there were at the dormitory when I returned. There must have been about ten of them sitting together, looking quite dejected. An older student who'd been living there for some time was in the middle of an impassioned monologue expressing indignation over the government's disloyalty in misleading the emperor, but nobody paid him much attention.

That evening, the teachers and students had a last dinner in the dormitory, and then sat together talking over all sorts of things. There was a sadness in the air, but at the same time a sense of liberation and relief. Many students expressed concern about the future of the university, which of course no one could foretell. The conversation soon turned to subjects like the fate of the military or estimations of the total number of fatalities in the city. The next day, we teachers were summoned to the university to attend a reading of the imperial rescript on the surrender. This ceremony was held in the small room formerly used by the air-raid precautions group, since it was the only room at the university that had not been burned. On the day of the bombing, the university president was visiting an area in the countryside to which some of the other students at Kazuko and Keiichi's school had been evacuated, so he was not hurt. But only a few members of the teaching staff were present, and many were injured. The president's voice choked with emotion, and he wiped tears from his eyes as he read. I myself was unmoved. I simply felt as if I were lying at the bottom of some tranquil, limpid body of water.

Afterward, I returned to the factory dormitory and sent the students under my charge back to their home towns. I then attended to some other unfinished business and stayed on at the dormitory that night. I finally returned to your bedside in Jigozen on the seventeenth.

The train I took was full of young demobilized sailors who were on their way home from the naval base in Kure. All of them carried huge cloth-wrapped parcels on their backs that contained their blankets, uniforms and their personal belongings. The movement of such demobilized personnel continued day after day for a long time, even after the Allied occupation forces arrived. While many sailors were leaving Kure at that time, very few military personnel boarded the trains at Hiroshima Station. This suggested to me how thoroughly the army in Hiroshima was decimated by the bombing.

As you know, the army was everything to Hiroshima. Many stories and rumors circulated about how the army was affected by the bombing; I don't know if these were true or not.

One story told of two or three hundred severely burned soldiers being laid out in rows, as if they were dead, and left completely unattended in the grounds of a national school in a town on the Kohin railroad line.

Another had the Eleventh Infantry Regiment, commonly known as the "Second Detachment," holding their induction

ceremony for new recruits when the flash occurred. Everyone
present was said to have been killed instantly, with the corpses
looking like a large catch of tuna hauled up on a beach. People
said the bodies were later doused with gasoline and set alight on
the spot. (Later I learned that the most basic fact was true—nearly
everyone there died. The new recruits were just entering the
gates and being checked against attendance lists when the flash
occurred, so the authorities apparently had a difficult time
answering queries about missing personnel.)

The military in Hiroshima was bereft of both leadership and
morale; surviving soldiers fled in all directions. Many people
reported seeing badly burned military personnel in ragged uniforms, wandering the hills and forests around the city.

I believe the authorities took every possible measure to round
up these men, but with little success. It is said, for instance, that
the Eleventh Infantry Regiment, a large number of whom were
local recruits, posted notices calling on its members to assemble at
Midorii village but that very few turned up. Some soldiers who
survived the bombing simply went home afterward, of their own
accord; when the time came for their demobilization, they were
of course nowhere to be found.

Another rumor had it that, in order to keep their huge losses a
secret, the army had quietly cremated or buried vast numbers of
soldiers. But as morale and military discipline were both very low,
this would have been very difficult to do. A former staff officer in
Hiroshima told me later that the army was concentrating all its
efforts at the time on simply saving lives, and his words had the
ring of truth.

Soldiers who participated in the rescue and clean-up operations were stationed in the areas surrounding Hiroshima at the time
of the bombing. Soldiers who arrived first and whose contribu-
tion was especially great were from a newly established regiment
located in the Haramura Parade Ground near Hachihonmatsu
Station.

The unfamiliar designations "Hiroshima Security Commander"

and "Army Marine Corps Commander" that I mentioned before referred to high-ranking emergency positions created after the bombing for security and rescue activities. The original Chugoku District Military Police headquarters was obliterated and its staff killed. You remember the army social club near the military police headquarters, right next to the school for children of military personnel? It is said that key officers of the Second Army's signal corps were attending a meeting there when the bomb was dropped, and that all were killed instantly.

Of course, such tragic incidents were not limited to the military, but one of the reasons for the large losses suffered by the army and associated personnel was that so many of their people were held up in Hiroshima due to the lack of transportation in the rapidly deteriorating war situation. As you know, virtually all inns and hotels in the city were being used exclusively to accommodate military personnel awaiting transfers and new assignments. Many dependents of servicemen were also waiting for passage to Manchuria, which was then considered to be the only safe haven from the impending "battle for mainland Japan." I believe that there were hundreds of such people trying to flee the city at that time.

Finally, I should tell you something about the organization of the army in Hiroshima at the time of the bombing and its state afterward.

While the First Army, with its headquarters in Tokyo, was responsible for defending eastern Japan in the event of an invasion, the Second Army, headquartered in Hiroshima, had authority for defense of western Japan (westward of the Suzuka mountain range). The Second Army was, of course, under the direct command of the imperial headquarters, as was the army marine headquarters in Ujina. The Chugoku District Military Police was under the command of the military police headquartered in Tokyo. The Second Army commanded the Chugoku District Army, which in turn was in charge of the Eleventh Infantry Regiment and the Fifth Artillery, Transport, Communications

and Engineering Regiments as well as the army hospitals. We all
knew there were ammunition depots, army clothing supply stores
and the like in the area. But we were totally unaware that the
headquarters for a newly formed division had been established in
the former Seventy-first Infantry Regiment compound of the
vacated army preparatory school in Hakushima and that a division commander had already been appointed.

We knew there were antiaircraft guns installed at the top of
Mount Futaba, as well as in Mukai-ujima and on the hill at the
back of Kusatsu; I am told that these were manned by operational
units of the Saku 8077 Corps under the command of the Third
Antiaircraft Division in Osaka. The Number Three Company
also had an installation. However, I heard that each of these was
equipped with only six antiaircraft guns. Given that a "military
center" like Hiroshima supposedly possessed a total of only twelve
or so antiaircraft guns to defend itself against possible attack by
massive formations of B-29s, it is certainly not surprising that a
couple of atomic bombs were able to bring the war to a close.

It has been estimated that there were at least fifteen thousand
military and related personnel in Hiroshima at the time of the
bombing. Many people think there were even more. Regardless,
the main army hospital and the Motomachi branch hospital were
instantly destroyed in the bombing, as were the headquarters of
the Second Army and the Chugoku District Army, as well as
facilities of the Military Police, the Eleventh Infantry Regiment,
the Fifth Artillery Regiment and the Fifth Transport Regiment.
It is estimated that at least two-thirds of their personnel were
either killed or wounded and Hiroshima's function as a military
center was indeed successfully cut off.

When you think about it, Hiroshima traces its development into
a military center back hundreds of years. It started out as capital of
the territory of the warlord Mori in the Age of Civil Wars, in the
fifteenth and sixteenth centuries. With the restoration of imperial
rule in the late nineteenth century, the existing army camps were

turned into army divisions. The imperial headquarters was located in Hiroshima during the time of the Sino-Japanese War (1894–1895). Then throughout the Russo-Japanese War (1904– 1905), World War I and World War II, Hiroshima continued to grow in importance and served as the gateway for the entire Japanese army.

Your home town and the place where we had lived as man and wife was wiped out as a military center, but it has not disappeared. The six deltas are still separated by seven sparkling rivers. Hiroshima is now being transformed from a military to a peace center. The tremendous sacrifice made there will be a silent warning to future generations. Fumiyo, I hope that you will find reason to bless our new city.

—May 30, 1946

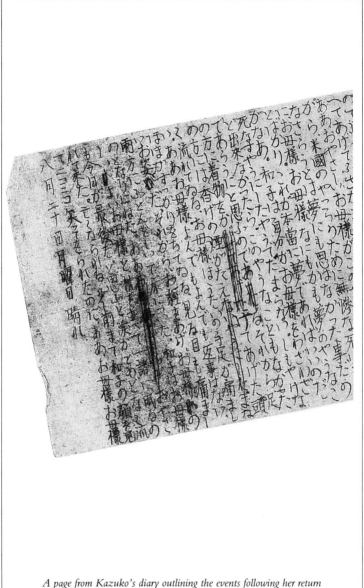

A page from Kazuko's diary outlining the events following her return to Hiroshima on August 18, 1945.

11

Radiation Sickness

August 17–20, 1945

Fumiyo,

I failed to realize how serious your condition was. While you were in the sickroom at the factory dormitory, I was tremendously relieved to see that you had somehow emerged from the ordeal with only minor burns. And when you mentioned the onset of untimely menstruation, I handed you one of my spare loincloths and simply attributed it to the trauma you had experienced. When I returned briefly to Jigozen on August 15, I was told that you had a high fever and were suffering from diarrhea. But I still wasn't unduly worried. From what little knowledge I had of medicine, I assumed that, from sleeping on the cold ground on the night of the tenth, you had caught a cold that affected your bowels. I wasn't all that worried about your lack of appetite either. To ease your anxiety, I told you that I would be back soon, permanently, to take good care of you. That was my firm intent when I left you to go back to the factory.

But when I returned to Setsuko's at about four p.m. on the seventeenth, you were terribly exhausted and emaciated. Soon your nose started to bleed, but you had always been prone to such bleeding, and with your continuing high fever, some bleeding from the nose didn't seem all that unusual. However, the bleeding wouldn't stop: when I gently pinched your nostrils, blood oozed from your mouth. And squeezing the nape of your neck didn't help. Blood kept gushing out of your nose and mouth, into a basin we had readied. You couldn't speak because of the bleeding. Then you moved your bandaged hand toward your chin and repeatedly made a gesture of scratching at your throat.

"What's the matter?" I asked.

"Here! Here!" you said in a whisper.

"What's wrong?"

"There's a ball stuck in here," you said with great difficulty.

I couldn't understand that at all. I just sat there, perplexed. But those words turned out to be about the last you would speak while in complete possession of your senses.

In the evening, Setsuko brought a doctor to the house. He was an acquaintance of your sister and her husband's who lived nearby. He had been working continuously at the Teishin (Postal Service) Hospital, treating victims of the bombing. He had just arrived home for the first time in six days when Setsuko begged him to come over and treat you. I explained your symptoms to him as best I could, whereupon he forcibly stuffed some gauze into your nostrils.

"Will that stop the bleeding?" I asked.

"I hope so," he said without much conviction.

He inserted his fingers into your mouth and pulled out a lump of dark reddish matter about the size of a bantam's egg. Then, to my surprise, he pulled out another.

"These are blood clots," he explained.

I then realized what you'd meant when you said that there was a ball stuck in your throat. The blood you were vomiting had coagulated in your throat, making your breathing labored and causing you great distress. You seemed to breathe a little more easily once the clots were removed from your throat. The bleeding stopped too. But I could hardly bring myself to look squarely at your pale, emaciated face, with its protruding cheekbones.

I asked the doctor about giving you a blood transfusion, but he said he had tried that on a number of patients without success. He also said something about the blood type's actually being altered, and about a drastic reduction in victims' white blood cell count. He had only very recently treated hundreds of patients with the same symptoms that you had. He mentioned that common symptoms included irregular menstruation, vomiting, lack of appetite, bleeding, diarrhea, extreme fatigue and high fever. He took your temperature and the thermometer read forty-one degrees centigrade. He said that most victims' temperatures ranged between forty and forty-two degrees. But there was no known treatment, and he offered no prognosis.

"Will she be all right?" I asked finally, but he didn't answer.

When he left, Setsuko actually ran out after him and repeated the question. She told me that his response was, "I don't think there's much hope." On hearing this, I almost passed out. All along, I had thought that you would eventually recover.

Your brother Tetsuji's family had already moved out of Setsuko's house and gone to live with relatives in the provinces. The back room they'd occupied in Setsuko's house was now your sickroom. I arranged Kinji's mattress next to yours and had him sleep beside you while I kept vigil by your bedside. There was nothing much I could do but apply a damp cloth to your forehead and chest, wringing it out periodically in a bucket of water brought from the kitchen. There was no ice whatsoever available. I felt your pulse by inserting my fingers under the bandage wrapped around your arm. Your heart was beating fast but there was nothing I could do about that. The only thing I could do was prevent mosquitoes from alighting on you or Kinji by chasing them away with a paper fan. Kinji was sound asleep, probably worn out from playing all day. His injuries had now healed completely. You also were fast asleep. After putting the children to bed, Setsuko joined me at your bedside. All was quiet. You didn't seem to be disturbed by the occasional steam or electric train that would rumble past the back of the house.

As there was nothing else to be done for the moment and you were resting calmly, I told Setsuko that she should get some sleep. The clock struck one. The electric trains had stopped running and the steam trains were now few and far between. It was completely quiet. I sat beside your bed, my mind numbed by the events of the day. Suddenly you opened your eyes and gazed up at me. You moved your lips, as if you were trying to say something. I bent over toward you but I couldn't hear anything. When I leaned back again, you raised your right hand and started to move it around in the air. Under the dim electric light, you moved your bandaged arm slowly up and down and from side to side. My stare alternated between your face and your moving hand.

You stopped and let your hand drop to your chest, as if you were tired. You seemed to be trying to say something with your eyes. I grew confused as you continued to stare.

"What's the matter?" I blurted out, almost reproachfully.

But you were quiet. After a while, you started moving your lips again, silently. You raised your right hand once more. Then I realized what you were trying to do.

You couldn't speak so you were forming characters in the air. I watched your hand carefully. It moved slowly, forming *katakana* characters with your hand! The movements were the same as before. At last, I was able to decipher the characters you were forming with your hand, "pencil and paper."

I nodded deeply in acknowledgment and said, "I understand. I understand."

You lowered your hand onto your breast and continued to gaze at me, your relief apparent.

I pulled out a notebook from my pocket, opened it to a blank page and put it into your left hand, the fingers of which were not bandaged. I inserted the pencil into a gap in the bandage covering your right hand. You brought both hands up onto your breast and paused for a moment. Then you began to write, shakily.

> *There are cans of sugar and candy in the bottom drawer of the second chest of drawers.*

You dropped your hands on your breast. After taking a few deep breaths, you continued.

There is flour and some powdered milk in the rice container.

You lowered your hands and closed your eyes. Then you opened them and gazed very pointedly at me. I was choking with emotion, but I forced a smile. You had no way to know that our house had been destroyed by fire, and you were concerned about the foodstuffs and sweets you had painstakingly set aside for the children. Finally, you raised your hands again and started writing again.

My love to Kazuko and Keiichi.

You let both hands drop onto your breast and closed your eyes. The notebook had slipped from your left hand. You seemed to have gone into a peaceful sleep. I took the notebook from you. Your awkward writing looked a first-grader's. Tears dropped from my eyes onto the notebook.

You seemed to be sleeping calmly now. Yet there had been something very unsettling about the intent gaze you had cast on me while ago. It had nothing to do with a foreboding of death. Rather, your gaze reminded me of the stare of a mentally unbalanced person. Visions of the two extremely agitated women I'd seen in the ruins on August 6 came to mind. I wondered if the high fever had affected your brain.

So the next morning, on the eighteenth, I asked your youngest brother Shiro, who was also there with us at Jigozen, to go and get Kazuko and Keiichi from the villages out in the country where they had gone with their classmates, and bring them back. We couldn't get a doctor to come to the house that day but I was sure now that the fever had done something to your brain. You smiled inanely when you opened your eyes, and uttered only incoherent phrases. You could speak now, which you had not been able to the night before, but this was a source of joy and sadness to me at the same time. Like a baby taking milk, you drank the fruit juice and sugared water that I fed you. I went to lie down for a while in the afternoon when Setsuko took over the vigil. When I woke up that evening, I found there had been no

change in your condition. At about eight o'clock, Shiro came
back with Kazuko and Keiichi.

Kazuko's diary of the last day she spent with you contains a
detailed account of what happened from that point.

> *When we stepped onto the porch at Aunt Setsuko's house,*
> *Father was standing there waiting for us. His left arm was sup-*
> *ported in a piece of white cloth slung around his neck. He said*
> *that Mother had gotten hurt when she was outside Fukuya's*
> *waiting for a train.*
>
> *The first time Father told her we were there she said,*
> *"What?" but the second time she said, "Oh, they are?" Her face*
> *was very thin.*
>
> *Kei-chan and I sat down on the floor side by side, right up*
> *near her head and greeted her.*
>
> *"Hello, Mother."*
>
> *She gazed at us for a while without saying anything.*
> *Father put his hand on my head and said, "Look, Kazuko is*
> *here."*
>
> *"You've gotten so big," she said. Then Father patted Kei-*
> *chan on the head and told Mother, "Keiichi too."*
>
> *"Oh yes, my little member of the 'smiling squad,'" Mother*
> *said. My teachers out in the country always made us smile*
> *a lot whenever they took group photographs to send our par-*
> *ents, so in her letters Mother always called my class the "smil-*
> *ing squad." She seemed to have gotten me and Kei-chan*
> *mixed up. I looked questioningly at Father. He lifted his*
> *hand to his forehead and told us that Mother's high fever had*
> *affected her head and that we should keep quiet. I suddenly*
> *felt very sad. Aunt Setsuko made dinner for us but I couldn't*
> *eat much.*
>
> *After dinner, Kei-chan and I went back to her room. Kei-*
> *chan fanned her face gently while I kept wetting down a hand*
> *towel and then squeezing it out and laying it on her forehead*
> *and chest. Father was sitting next to her. Kin-chan was*

grumpy because Kei-chan wouldn't play with him, but pretty soon he lay down beside Mother and fell asleep.

In the meantime Father, who had been checking Mother's pulse, noticed something strange. So he called Aunt Setsuko and Uncle Shiro, and everybody came into the room. Mother opened her eyes wide and said, "What are you doing here? What happened? What do you want?" I couldn't hold back my tears.

Then Father brought out a photo of baby Toshiko and showed it to Mother, asking, "Do you know who this is?"

"It's Toshiko," Mother said clearly.

Then I showed her a picture of Kenji Miyazawa.*

She looked at it and said "Kenji-chama," in a baby voice.

Tears started falling from my eyes again. Father's eyes were full of tears too.

Mother went on. "Let's go together into the blue sky. Let's hurry off to Hanamaki. Did you find out yet where Polan Plaza is? Let's hurry and ride on the Milky Way railroad!"

I thought she might be a little better now, because when she saw the photo of Kenji Miyazawa it reminded her of what we used to say about his stories.

But Father said, "She's really lightheaded."

This made me sad again and I tried hard to cool Mother's forehead and chest. Suddenly she opened her eyes and looked right at me, and said in a scolding tone, "It's late. Off to bed." When I realized Mother was worried about us even though she was so sick herself, I started to cry again. I went out in the kitchen to get a fresh bucket of water and then kept on cooling off Mother's forehead and chest. Soon she fell into a calm sleep.

"She seems to be a bit more stable now. Everybody please go and get some rest," Father said.

---

* [The author wrote several books of literary criticism on the humanist poet and children's writer Kenji Miyazawa (1896–1933), in the course of which both he and his family developed a close relationship with Miyazawa's family.]

*Aunt Setsuko and Uncle Shiro left and went off to bed.
Then Father said to us, "You must be tired. Go to bed now."
Kei-chan lay down beside Kin-chan and fell asleep. I stayed
up a while longer, but since Father kept insisting, I finally lay
down beside Kei-chan. But I couldn't get to sleep at first. I
remember hearing the clock strike three.*

Each time you opened your eyes that night, you muttered something senseless. One time, you gazed at the children sleeping and
said, "Ye pathetic ones," almost as if it was Christ speaking. I
wondered whether you were in your right mind.

Your condition was more or less the same on the nineteenth.
Masako, from Kure, who had looked after you with Setsuko while
I was off at the factory, came to visit. Your brother, Hideichi,
came from Kanayacho and of course Setsuko and Shiro were with
you constantly. I wonder how many of the tens of thousands of
people who died as a result of the bombing were able to spend
their last moments at home in their own bed, surrounded by family, as you were. In this sense you were blessed. You were delirious
now, saying things like, "There's a mountain of sugar to the east.
Let's bake a cake with lots of milk and flour." And when I called
out "Fumiyo! Fumiyo!" to bring you to your senses, you'd frown
and say, "Shh! So noisy!" Or you'd laugh and say to the children,
"You're lucky to have such a funny papa." Your remarks had
the unintended effect of brightening up the depressing atmosphere of the sickroom. In the meantime, you drank all the fruit
juice and sugared water I gave you. In the afternoon, you passed a
lot of blood in your stool and urine. You let me clean you up and
I was reminded how emaciated you had become. Sometime in
the late afternoon a big roundworm came out of your mouth. I
had seen such worms crawling out of the mouths of some of the
corpses I had come across in the days after the bombing.
Apparently the worms could no longer exist in the decaying
internal organs of the victims and were abandoning their hosts.

From about that time, your condition rapidly deteriorated, but all I could do was to keep on checking your pulse. Finally, at eight-thirty in the evening, your heart stopped beating. There was no doctor available even in your last moments.

Our three children and I cleansed your body in preparation for your funeral. We had no new bandages, so we left the old ones in place. On removing your clothing, I was astonished to see for the first time how badly your shoulders and waist had been bruised. You had never once complained about any pain from such bruises, though I did often feel that your movements were sluggish for someone whose burns were relatively minor and who was normally so strong-willed. The pain from the bruises must have been restricting your movements.

Forgive me, Fumiyo. I didn't realize how badly you were suffering. I don't deny that it was because of my own ignorance and inadequate attention to you. But I wasn't the only one who was ignorant. Even medical specialists didn't know the cause of the sickness afflicting so many survivors. The term "radiation sickness" was not part of the medical vocabulary of the time. So when I went to obtain a death certificate the next day, the doctor listed the cause of death as "heart failure." This was probably standard procedure then.

On the evening of August 19, I asked Setsuko to make the necessary arrangements for the wake. After I offered some Buddhist prayers, the children and I recited Kenji Miyazawa's best-known poem, "Standing Up to the Rain" all together, just like we used to do at home before the Buddhist altar when you were alive.* We did the same thing the next day when people from the neighborhood gathered to pay their last respects. In fact, it would have been impossible to find a Buddhist priest to perform the funeral service, even if we had wanted to. As a result, your funeral was not conducted according to Christian, Shinto or Buddhist rites. Rather, it turned out to be based on a literary work by Kenji Miyazawa. I'm sure you were pleased with it.

---

* [See page 193.]

On the night of the wake, I asked everyone to retire early and used the big mosquito net for the first time in three days. Then we all lay together, the five of us, side by side, as we often had when you were alive. You always used to say, especially in the last few years, that you didn't think you would be able to keep pace with me in life, and that you would like to die in my arms when the time came. So I held your rigid, cold body in my arms till morning.

Your funeral took place on August 20, which was also my birthday. The timing must have been one of those "strange quirks of fate" you often used to talk about. When I went to the Jigozen village office to notify them of your death and to get permission to have your remains cremated, there were lots of people lined up at the counter, almost as if they were waiting for food rations or cigarette quotas. Many who had been staying with relatives or friends in Jigozen or who had managed to make their way to the relief station set up at the local school were now dying of the same ailment as you had.

As a result, the crematorium was terribly congested. It was a small town, and the facility had only two furnaces. So holes had been dug in the ground around it, and corpses were being cremated in the open air. As coffins too were in short supply, they were being used over and over again. A corpse would be taken out of its coffin upon arrival at the crematorium and the same coffin would then be used to bring in another corpse. You were taken to the crematorium in this same way, but your departure was attended by your immediate family and your relatives and the people from the neighborhood. And you were cremated in one of the furnaces.

It was rare, at the time, for a cremation to be attended by so many people. There were usually only one or two relatives present, and cremations were often conducted by people who were complete strangers to the deceased. Therefore yours was truly a "grand" funeral. You were one of those rare people who are blessed in their final days. You deserved at least this much for having put up with such an intractable husband and for being such a good person all your life.

Considerable progress has since been made in research on radiation sickness, which was the cause of your death.

I think I wrote before that the symptoms are caused by radioactivity, which is emitted at the time of nuclear fission, and are the same as those seen in cases of overexposure to radium or X-rays. The most conspicuous symptoms are caused by drastic reductions in the number of red and white blood cells. The reduced number of white corpuscles, especially, retards the healing of wounds and burns. These consequently fester and suppurate, shrouding the living victim in the odor of a corpse. The odor of death that accompanied the mortally wounded victims I came across at rescue stations and other places was no doubt due to this condition. You were probably also in this state.

Bleeding from the gums and the mucous membranes throughout the mouth, nostrils and throat was a common symptom, which explained the blood that had come from your nose and mouth later. Radiation also interfered with the functioning of your internal organs and caused internal bleeding. Your untimely menstruation, vomiting and passing of blood, high fever, diarrhea, anemia, loss of appetite and fatigue were all symptoms. No doubt your white blood cell count was drastically low too.

By the way, I believe that the effective range of the radiation was not as great as that of the accompanying air blast or the thermal rays. Take the case of your sister, Aiko, for instance. Although she was hit by the blast and sustained burns from the heat rays, she wasn't apparently affected by radiation. Her burns were much more serious than yours, but they got better rapidly and she suffered no complications. According to investigations carried out by experts, the effective range of the radiation was generally less than that of the air blast or the heat rays, but the relationship between distance and radiation dosage proved to be very inconsistent.

Some victims who were further away from the explosion suffered to a greater extent from radiation than people who were closer. Generally speaking, however, people who were near the hypocenter were exposed to radiation, while those who were more than about three kilometers away were not. Being indoors at the time afforded no protection, since radiation, unlike the blast or the heat rays, penetrates solid objects. Actually, Setsuko's husband's aunt from Hirosecho is a good example. She managed to crawl out unhurt from the debris of her crushed house and went to an emergency site on the delta of the Tenma River. Then she got a lift and was able to make her way home. About the same time that you were ill in bed, she was running a high fever too, and suffering from severe diarrhea.

She was in bed for more than two months but finally made a full recovery. However, she had spots all over her body and had lost all her hair. The appearance of these spots and the loss of hair were very common symptoms at the time. I believe that the spots were caused by bleeding under the skin. Many people who showed these symptoms never recovered.

Lots of people who entered the city of Hiroshima after the day of the bombing also developed the same symptoms and eventually died. I believe this was because they walked through areas containing large amounts of residual radioactivity. According to one study, of the approximately 100,000 people who died, 75,000, or seventy-five percent, died on the sixth, and 15,000, or fifteen percent, died within two weeks, between August 7 and 20. These represent the victims of the first phase of radiation sickness. The remaining 10,000 people, or ten percent, died during the period August 21–October 16, or between the third and eighth weeks. These were victims of the second phase of the disease; it's said that most people who survived this phase eventually recovered. You were one of victims who succumbed at the end of the first phase, while Setsuko's husband's aunt from Hirosecho survived the second phase and recovered.

Of the 100,000 dead, the 75,000 killed on the day of the bombing were not victims of the disease. Most were crushed when their houses collapsed. Of course, many were killed by the blast or were trapped under debris and incinerated in the fires that followed. Many who were rescued or managed to free themselves succumbed later to injuries and burns.

As I mentioned, almost none of these mortally wounded people were able to receive medical treatment that same day. So, it can generally be said that most people killed on August 6 were the victims of wounds and burns, while those who died later were victims of radiation sickness. In any case, whatever the direct or the indirect cause of death—external injuries were the result of the blast; burns were caused by heat rays; the disease that killed you was caused by radiation—all these were of course effects of the atomic bomb.

At the risk of repeating myself, I would like to summarize what I have observed about injuries and burns. As I mentioned, external wounds were caused mainly by the air blast accompanying the explosion: many people were killed or injured when buildings collapsed on them. Victims who were not killed at that time sustained injuries such as lacerations, bruises, sprains, broken bones or being showered with flying glass fragments. Such victims were generally inside at the time. Many people who were outdoors at locations near the hypocenter were flung to the ground and died instantly. The abdomens of some victims burst open, their intestines spilling out onto the ground. Some people's eyeballs popped out of their sockets. Your bruises, although they fell into this category of injury, were relatively light. There were many cases in which people more than four kilometers from the hypocenter still sustained injuries when they were knocked to the ground by the blast.

One member of the university staff was blown out through the door to his room, hurled into the room opposite and dashed against the wall on the far side of that room. But he suffered only minor injuries. Had he been smashed against the wall of his own room, he would probably have been killed instantly. Some of the most common and visually horrifying external injuries were caused by glass fragments. People with these injuries often bled heavily and had pieces of broken glass sticking out all over their bodies. Some were blinded; others had ears or noses severed. Many victims eventually recovered, with dozens of small glass fragments still embedded in their skin. Apparently not many died solely as a result of this type of injury.

The number of people burned by the heat rays was far greater among those who were outside than those who were inside, and the burns suffered outdoors were much more severe as well. Almost invariably, people who were burned by heat rays while indoors were near windows. On the other hand, people who were outside but had been shielded from the flash by some object, including clothing, were not burned. It appears that people who were within about three kilometers of the hypocenter sustained burns on any parts of their bodies that were exposed. As was the case with external injuries caused by the blast, the closer a victim was to the hypocenter, the greater the severity of the burns from the flash. Strangely, while black clothing was sometimes scorched and the skin beneath it burned, white clothing was usually not. I have heard stories too about the white background on the timetables posted up at railroad stations remaining untouched while the black lettering was scorched.

In the outskirts of Koi, I saw a rice paddy in which the crop had been seared white except for a small portion shielded by a house. This part, in the shape of the shadow formed by the house when the flash occurred, was as green as ever. Damage to plant life seemed to extend for a considerable distance from the hypocenter, but as most of the trees on Hijiyama Hill and Mount Futaba began to sprout new leaves again soon afterward, apparently the effects were not long-term.

I heard a strange story about two passengers who were on a train waiting to depart from Hiroshima Station. As I might have mentioned when I was telling you about Aiko's burns, victims were usually unaware they had been burned until later, when the swelling and inflammation started. These two passengers were seated facing each other on the south side of the carriage. One closed the window on his side, while the other left his open. Just then they were assailed by the blast and the heat of the explosion. The passenger who had closed his window was wounded by shards of glass and soon covered in blood. The passenger who'd left his window open was not evidently injured. He immediately put the bleeding passenger on his back and hurried off with him to the East Parade Ground. But soon he was the one writhing in pain as his heat ray burns grew inflamed. Now it was the blood-soaked passenger's turn to look after him.

—June 20, 1946

Stone, carved with a poem by Kenji Miyazawa, dedicated to the repose of the Ogura family ancestors.

Lingering Fears

August–September, 1945

Fumiyo,

During the period from about two weeks before to two weeks after your death, Japan experienced greater change and turmoil than it had ever undergone before. These were triggered mainly by Japan's surrender on August 15. But even this social upheaval did not directly affect the lives of the survivors of the bombing to any large extent.

The entry of the American occupation forces into Hiroshima was a case in point. More than a few people in Hiroshima were eagerly awaiting the troops' arrival. As you know, people in Hiroshima have more relatives and friends living in America than do people from any other area of the country. Many of those expatriates were now citizens of the United States and a considerable number had joined that country's armed forces; surely some would come to Hiroshima. There had been no word from many of them in the previous four or five years. Servicemen coming from America would at least bring the latest news. Hopes and expectations like these constituted a bright spot in the lives of people who had loved ones in America.

You were always worried about your uncle and his family and others you knew who had emigrated to America. Unfortunately, there's no news yet of your uncle and his family or of your friends. But since the occupation troops arrived, the atmosphere in the city has grown brighter than anyone would have thought possible during the war. The children have taken to the American soldiers and are very friendly with them. Quite a few people are being visited by relatives or friends from the United States who are now members—or in some cases officers—of the armed forces. They all report that Japanese people in America are as happy and prosperous as they were before the war. So I think you can rest assured that your uncle and his family are doing fine over there. One sight that I've been happy to see since the surrender is that of Japanese-American servicemen walking cheerfully side by side with local people.

On the other hand, radiation sickness soon plunged survivors into a state of morbid anxiety about their health. People's concern is apparent even now, almost a year later.

There seemed to be no limit to what the disease could do: many people survived it for a time, only to succumb later, while many who were only slightly injured in the blast or who entered the city soon afterward to search for relatives and friends died later, after returning home. Rumors soon began to spread, that people who'd walked across the East Parade Ground were doomed or that poison gas had permeated the soil at the hypocenter.

An article that appeared in the newspaper on August 24 helped to fuel such rumors. Its boldface headline proclaimed, "The atomic bomb's legacy of fear—Hiroshima uninhabitable for 75 years." The article stressed that burns sustained by victims were not ordinary burns and that people's blood corpuscles had been destroyed by the characteristic action of uranium, leading first to extreme difficulty in breathing and then to an agonizing death. People said that for the next seventy-five years both Hiroshima and Nagasaki would be unfit to sustain any life—animal or vegetable. It concluded by noting that there had been calls for preserving the ruins of Hiroshima and Nagasaki as is, after the manner of Pompei, as the most eloquent peace memorials possible.

This article generated considerable concern throughout the country, but you can imagine the shock it caused within

Hiroshima at the time. People's families, relatives and acquaintances were dying almost daily, and practically everyone had walked on ground that was contaminated by radioactivity. I must confess I was greatly worried myself, and was especially concerned about future health problems Kinji might have.

The fallacy of the idea that Hiroshima and Nagasaki would not support life for seventy-five years was exposed by a statement issued on September 12 in Nagasaki by a member of a scientific team headed by U.S. Brigadier General Farrell, charged with documenting the effects of the bombs dropped on Hiroshima and Nagasaki. I saw the statement for the first time in the newspaper of September 17, but it was only a small news item and it gave no particular instructions or precautions. No wonder people's fears ran away with them.

The results of the first so-called "scientific study" of the bombing's effects were summarized in the paper of August 24 in the form of a site survey report by the Air Defense Headquarters. Yet this report made no mention whatsoever of radiation sickness. It was not until September that the Japanese government finally mobilized all the available scientists in the country and organized a large-scale investigation. A special committee headed by the Scientific Research Conference was also established to survey damage and casualties. Its first meeting was held on September 14 in Tokyo University's engineering department. But their discussions proceeded at such a slow pace that the survey team of two hundred or so members did not even leave for Hiroshima and Nagasaki until about September 20.

I first began to understand something about radiation sickness on September 19 when one of the newspapers carried a report that the former principal of the military medical college had submitted to the special committee.

This report stated that while the dormant period of radiation sickness and the disease's severity upon manifestation both depended primarily on the amount of radiation to which one was exposed, the progress of the disease was greatly influenced by a person's living conditions. An essential part of treatment was having the patient conserve his or her energy by getting adequate rest, avoiding stress and eating nutritious food. But of course circumstances in the city made it difficult to fulfill any of these conditions. Besides, survivors without apparent injuries and those who were hurt only slightly tended to overexert themselves in reconstruction work. As a result, many of these people later succumbed to the disease.

I'm sure Professor Kurita and his family's ability to overcome the disease was related to their strict adherence to this regimen's basic points. He had lived in Nagaregawa, in the central part of the city. As I wrote before, when I went there on August 6, I found his house had been consumed by fire and that it was impossible even to approach the site because of the heat. I was afraid Professor Kurita and his family might have been killed but I found out later that they were all safe except for the daughter, the schoolteacher whom I mentioned previously. All the other family members were inside the house when it collapsed but fortunately were able to extricate themselves before the fire broke out. All were wounded, but Professor and Mrs. Kurita the most seriously. The family hastily sought refuge at Sentei Park, but the conflagration soon caught up with them there. So they waded across the river to Nigitsu and went on from there to Ushiba, where they were able to stay with a friend.

I guess it was on August 9, when I was returning from the university that I visited them. Although Professor Kurita's friend, a Mr. Goto, had been slightly wounded, the other members of Mr. Goto's family were fine and his house was not damaged. I remember thinking at the time the whole family looked listless and unhealthy, particularly Professor Kurita and his wife. As you know, he is almost obsessive about his health, and shortly after I visited, he and his family moved way out to Kisamachi, where he found a sympathetic doctor. The whole family received regular nutrient injections, took adequate meals and settled down to a quiet, uneventful routine.

But my concern for him mounted as the problem of radiation sickness came to light. His house was about the same distance from the hypocenter as Fukuya's, where you had been standing. Entire families were wiped out in his neighborhood. And Sentei Park, where his family took refuge, was very close to the center of the blast. So they were definitely exposed to large amounts of radiation for a considerable length of time. Yet when I visited him at his retreat in the country a month later, I was very surprised. He and his whole family had recovered completely. I was even able to tell him lightheartedly how worried I had been about their health. I'm sure that his attention to health concerns was what saved them.

I believe that specialists from the United States are stationed now at the Red Cross Hospital in Hiroshima to study radiation sickness and that Japanese doctors are engaged in similar research. Surely they will all help us to learn more as soon as possible about this disease. The director of the Hiroshima Red Cross Hospital wrote somewhere that the single-minded way in which these specialists—particularly those from the United States—were conducting their research was highly commendable.

Speaking of this hospital, it was the first medical facility to resume work on August 6, and it provided the greatest amount of help and comfort to the victims. Although the Teishin (Postal Service) Hospital in Hakushima, which is where the doctor who treated you worked, resumed aid activities immediately after the bombing too and did excellent work, it stood at some remove from the city center and, because it was intended primarily for postal workers, was not that well known among the general public. The Red Cross Hospital was probably the first one that sprang to mind for many of the survivors who flocked there.

Yet the Red Cross Hospital, like other facilities, sustained heavy damage and suffered enormous casualties among its personnel. But unlike some governmental departments and agencies, this hospital never once suspended its activities. Despite great difficulties, it continued to assist the sick and wounded, in the true Red Cross spirit.

Fortunately, as houses around the hospital had been removed
to create firebreaks, the approach of fire was slow. Still, the student nurses' dormitory behind the main building was leveled and
burned, and the degree of destruction inside the main building
and the patient wards was similar to that which our university had
sustained. That the hospital escaped conflagration was due to the
heroic fire fighting efforts of staff, nurses and patients. They say
that the work of the young nurses—most of whom were themselves wounded—was truly astounding. The hospital was fortunate too to have a large number of navy and army personnel
among its patients, and a naval rescue party that landed near Meiji
Bridge soon after the bombing also provided assistance.

These people were able to save the main building and the
patient wards from the ravages of fire. But the interior was wrecked
by the force of the blast and was strewn with debris. Medical
equipment was totally destroyed and supplies spilled and scattered
beyond salvage. Nurses were dispatched to the army marine
corps' clinic in Ujina, but it too was running short of medicines
and drugs. I believe the nurses came back with just a bottle of
mercurochrome.

Only a few of the surviving doctors and nurses were healthy
enough to work. Most patients urgently required surgery, and yet
any individualized care whatsoever was out of the question.
Doctors and nurses merely sterilized wounds with hydrogen per-
oxide and applied mercurochrome. Bandages were also in short
supply, so if wounds were judged to be minor, the old bandages
were reapplied. In most of the grave cases, the best that could be
done was merely to give patients some water in their final
moments. At night there was no electricity and in the dim glow
of candlelight, steel helmets were handed out to the seriously
wounded patients for use as chamber pots. To dispose of the
mounting number of dead, holes were dug in the vacant lots
around the building and corpses were cremated in these holes in
the open air, just as was done in the crematorium.

However, as rescue teams and medical supplies began to arrive from the military and other sources, hospital staff started working around the clock. After some weeks, the day-to-day running of the hospital had stabilized enough that research on the dreaded radiation sickness could get underway.

As I said, anxiety about the disease was not limited to residents of Hiroshima and its immediate environs. After your funeral I took Kazuko and Keiichi back to Saijo which, as you know, is located in the mountains near the northeastern end of Hiroshima Prefecture. This was around the beginning of September. It's about a half a day's journey by train.

Yet even some people from that remote area who'd visited Hiroshima after the bombing later developed the symptoms of radiation sickness and eventually died. No doubt they'd walked through highly radioactive areas. On their return to the country-side, many complained of feeling tired, but thought that they were just suffering from fatigue as a result of their exertions. They took time off from work and rested at home but in the meantime developed fevers, loose bowels and spots on the skin, all of which gradually got worse. I heard many such anecdotes from people on trains, in the town of Saijo and in nearby villages.

The disease is said to remain dormant for long periods in some cases, and to recur even after apparently being cured in others. Lingering fears do still trouble survivors, but I imagine that these will eventually subside. But the numerical data on the casualties and damage will stand as a permanent reminder of the cataclysm.

It should be pointed out though, that the integrity of the data available is compromised by the fact that all the government agencies possessing the basic information necessary for any such surveys were obliterated. In addition, reports at the time set the total number of corpses buried or cremated by police or military authorities at 32,959, yet innumerable burned bones of numerous human beings are still being uncovered in the ruins, a year after the bombing. Figures that seem to be precise should in fact be understood as only approximate.

The results of surveys carried out by the prefectural authorities on August 12, less than one week after the bombing, calculated the dead at 30,000, the missing at 22,000, the gravely wounded at 24,000 and the wounded at 81,000. But as large numbers of wounded continued to die, the total probably rose soon thereafter to 70,000 or 80,000. Another report estimated 60,000 to 70,000 dead and over 100,000 wounded, with the total number of people affected by the bombing exceeding 200,000. Of course these were based on rough estimates.

Because of the rate at which people were dying, data on the number of fatalities varied greatly depending on the date on which a survey was conducted. I have heard that three clerks from the census section of the city offices resumed their duties at the former residence of Rai Sanyo on Hijiyama Hill on August 15. And as of November 1, they set the number of dead at 75,000, of whom 38,000 were male and 37,000 female.

The most comprehensive statistics on casualties are probably those contained in the report submitted to the GHQ on February 2 of this year (1946), which reads:

	MALE	FEMALE	INDETERMINATE	SUM
Dead	38,756	37,065	2,329	78,150
Missing	7,031	6,952		13,983
Gravely wounded	4,818	4,610		9,428
Wounded	13,541	14,456		27,997
Property loss				176,987
Total affected				306,545

The missing may well be considered dead, so by this account fatalities number 92,133, while the total wounded, gravely or otherwise, is 37,425. Total dead and wounded then amounts to 129,558.

The actual population of the city at the time of the bombing is, unfortunately, unknown. Although a figure of 265,000 is often cited, I think that this was estimated on the basis of the number of people registered for food rationing, which was probably 245,000, plus about 20,000 commuters from other districts and people passing through at the time. But something is clearly wrong with this population estimate, since it is substantially lower than the number of total affected persons given in the report to the GHQ. I suspect that military and related personnel were not included in this figure. I personally think that there were at least 360,000 to 370,000—probably as many as 400,000—people in Hiroshima that day. Assuming that the number was 400,000, then three-fourths of the people in the city were directly affected in some way. Over one-quarter of the population was killed or wounded, with the number of dead higher than the number of injured.

My estimate of the population at the time is based on the number of dwellings as reported in surveys conducted by the city offices before the bombing. I believe that there were 78,838 units as of June 1944. This had fallen to 74,215 by July 1945, as houses were demolished for firebreaks from April 1945. Assuming that each household had five members, the population would have been approximately 370,000. I don't think this estimate is excessive.

The city gives the numbers of homes that were destroyed or damaged as follows:

	COMPLETE	PARTIAL	SUM
Fire destruction	55,000	2,290	57,290
Blast destruction	6,820	3,750	10,570
Total destruction by fire or blast	61,820	6,040	67,860

Here, houses completely destroyed by fire include those which were completely or partially leveled and then consumed by fire, while houses totally destroyed by the blast are those that were leveled but did not burn. Houses that were leveled and then also burned were generally located within a radius of two kilometers of the hypocenter. Partially destroyed or partially burned houses lay outside this circle, as a rule.

In any case, 61,820 dwellings had disappeared. Moreover, the 6,040 partially burned or partially leveled houses were uninhabable. Subtracting the sum of these figures—67,860—from the 74,215 dwellings existing in April 1945 leaves just 6,355 dwellings after the bombing—less than one-tenth of the number that had stood before.

It is estimated that about 85,000 people lived in the 6,000-odd dwellings left standing. Yet this entire population was scattered around the outskirts of the city, as the area within two kilometers of the hypocenter was uninhabitable. The term "atomic desert," which came into vogue at that time, was certainly apt. It is estimated that about 130,000 people took refuge in nearby provinces immediately after the bombing; of these, about twenty percent are thought to have died later of radiation sickness.

Large numbers of evacuees are now beginning to return to the city and as a result, this desert is being repopulated at a remarkable pace. Hiroshima residents numbered 169,000 in February this year, 179,000 in May and about 186,000 as of July 20. Of course, these numbers include demobilized servicemen and people returning from former Japanese colonies. Still the increase is mainly on the outskirts rather than near the hypocenter. For example, there are just 621 school-age children living in the Otemachi school district near the hypocenter, while there are 16,500 children of this age in the Ujina school district, which sustained almost no casualties or destruction.

Only about 6,500 people now live in the area that was formerly the city center. There are 34,000 within a radius of one to two kilometers of the center, 70,000 people within two to three kilometers, and 75,000 people at a distance of more than that. This should give you a good idea of the state of desolation at the hypocenter.

—July 30, 1946

The Thinker

1945–1946

Fumiyo,

Today is August 6. It was one year ago that you collapsed in front of the Fukuya department store. A citizens' rally for the reconstruction of Hiroshima and a memorial service for those who died were held this morning on Jisenjibana—the area of the delta right near the hypocenter. I just came home after attending both, and am now stripped to the waist, trying to cool off. It was almost as hot in the city today as it was a year ago.

But it's cool here at your sister's place in Jigozen, near the coast. I'm living in their storehouse now. As you know, we borrowed their back room as your sickroom in your final days. After you were gone, I asked them to lend me the second floor of the small storehouse in their backyard. I don't think you were ever up here. It's like an attic, about the size of a six-mat room, with unplaned floorboards over which I've laid some coarse tatami mats. I've nailed boards on the east window in place of the panes that were destroyed by the blast. I also received the items that you so carefully packed and sent ahead to the provinces as emergency supplies in case of air raids. And so, almost a year ago I began living in this storehouse with the three children. It was not a life to which I was accustomed. I have felt as helpless as a male bird looking after three fledglings without its mate.

I light a few sticks of incense and set them into a plain, ash-filled porcelain bowl in front of the urn that holds your ashes, on top of the overturned box I use as a makeshift altar. As I gaze at the fine, wavering stream of smoke, I wonder how it can be that I have survived an entire year. The thought depresses me and makes me feel that I must write to you. So in a departure from my usual custom, I've decided to write this letter now, during the day.

It's almost nine months since I first started writing. I've counted the letters, and this one is the thirteenth. I've outlined my experiences from the moment of the explosion at 8:15 on the morning on August 6 last year through the moment of your death on the night of the nineteenth. I've briefly described how a single bomb completely changed the face of your home town and told you all I know about the fates of your dearly beloved brothers and sisters, relatives and friends.

I've recently come to associate the destruction of Hiroshima with the fiery end of Sodom and Gomorrah.

You may recall the verses from Genesis which read:

"Then the Lord rained upon Sodom and upon Gomorrah brimstone and fire from the Lord out of heaven; and he overthrew those cities, and all the valley, and all the inhabitants of the cities, and what grew on the ground."*

Hiroshima could well be called the Sodom and Gomorrah of Japan because of its lengthy development along imperialistic lines. Hiroshima seems to have been destined to become a military center ever since the castle-building days of the feudal lords Mori and Asano; certainly its development and modernization beginning in the late nineteenth century were undertaken for the sole purpose of increasing its military power. Even the peculiar Choshu dialect that military personnel used when introducing themselves has become a part of the vernacular of Hiroshima. The Choshu district in neighboring Yamaguchi Prefecture was noted for the many high-ranking army officers it produced during the late nineteenth and early twentieth centuries. I can't help feeling that

---

* [Genesis 19:24 (Revised Standard Version).]

Hiroshima slowly wove the fabric of its own destiny, fashioning itself over the years into a target for the atomic bomb.

On the night of September 17, just over a month after its fiery destruction, Hiroshima was deluged with rain reminiscent of the Flood of Noah's time. The entire Chugoku district was hit by the biggest typhoon the area had seen in at least a dozen years.

About ten bridges had already been destroyed in the bombing. On September 17, another twenty were washed away by flood-waters. Hiroshima was not only the city of water; it was also the city of bridges, as you well know. Now, with so many of its bridges gone, small boats were in use everywhere, ferrying people across the rivers, as in bygone days. There was no ferry service at the spot previously spanned by Asahi Bridge, so you either had to wade across or make a long detour to Koi Bridge to get to the university from Koi. Nishi-ohashi Bridge was oddly deformed but still in place. Ferry boats were in service at the Kan'on and Sumiyoshi bridges where the river was too deep to cross on foot, even at low tide. People waited while a single small boat plied back and forth, so it took about two hours to travel a distance that would have taken only twenty minutes by train.

Many who were lucky enough to survive the bombing now saw their houses destroyed by the typhoon and their possessions washed away by the floodwaters. This happened to young Ikeda, a student who had fled to the village of Kumura, ten kilometers from the city. The winds took practically all the temporary shacks that people had erected in the ruins after the bombing, including that of your uncle Yoshimura. People in the surrounding areas like Koi and Minami who'd narrowly escaped the fires after the bombing and had since been taking shelter in the wreckage of their homes now lost everything. Some people fled to outlying areas at that point, while others had no alternative but to rebuild their flimsy shacks on the same sites. When I think of these people, I feel that we were very fortunate to have secured the use of this storehouse early on. Compared with the shanties dotting the scorched ground, our temporary abode is a palace.

For some time after the typhoon, the bare landscape reinforced my idea that Hiroshima had first suffered the same fate as Sodom and Gomorrah and then been inundated by another Flood.

The atomic desert created by forces unleashed by modern science was quickly transformed by the fury of the elements into a primeval ice field. Seeing this, I used to muse that when human civilization came to an end, all vestiges of the present age and the ages past would be obliterated by the forces of nature and that the earth would return to a primordial state. Lately, though, I have begun to think a little more practically about the future destinies of the city and its people.

I wouldn't go so far as to call us lucky, but the three children and I did survive both the holocaust and the flood. Actually I became separated from the children after the typhoon and lost all contact with them for about a month. However, after a great deal of frantic searching, I eventually found them, and miraculously enough they were not harmed. We are now living together again in this storehouse. Today, looking back over the past year, I feel that everyone has a different destiny to fulfill and that the people who survived must have been fated to do so, like Lot and Noah and their families.

Of course I realize that all this sounds old-fashioned, but when I see the way Japan is being reborn after the surrender under the Allied—especially the American—military occupation, I can't help thinking that the conflagration and flood were God's way of doing away with the old Japan and baptizing the new. I keep thinking of Nietzche's statement that history can be borne only by the stouthearted. Though we may not possess the stout hearts of Lot or Noah, I believe that we must make an effort to trust in the destiny that is written for us. I earnestly hope that our three children will be, all their lives, "as wise as serpents and as innocent as doves."*

I must tell you about one more thing in the ruins of Hiroshima.

---

* [Matthew 10:16 (Revised Standard Version).]

It concerns the stone steps at the entrance of the Kamiyacho branch of the Sumitomo Bank. If you face the steps and look down at the right-hand corner, you see that that area is noticeably darker than the rest. Actually, the entire facade of the building is now much lighter in color than when you were alive. The whole surface underwent a tremendous and instantaneous physical change, because of the heat rays. Just before the explosion, someone was sitting on one of the lower steps, taking a rest, apparently with an elbow propped on his knee and his chin lowered onto his cupped hand. Then came the blinding flash, followed by intense heat. No doubt the person was killed instantly, as he was just four or five hundred meters from the hypocenter. But an indelible shadowlike image was formed on the part of the stone steps that was shielded from the flash by his body.

I first learned of this from Mr. Toriyama, a lecturer in earth science at the university. He said that the shadow on the steps brought to mind the image of a Roman soldier in the ruins of Pompei. When I saw it though, I immediately thought of Rodin's sculpture of a man deep in thought. As you know, I like that work so much that I always had a photo of it hanging on the wall of my study, and took it along each time we moved to a new place. The photo was of course lost in the fire, but it sprang to mind when I saw the image on the steps. From the moment I saw that shadow, it became for me a new incarnation of the "thinker."

Every time I catch sight of the shadow from a streetcar window or while passing by on foot, a chill runs through my body. That murky image compels the viewer to think about the fate of mankind.

The problems stemming from the invention of the atomic bomb are countless. I detest the use of atomic bombs in war; I hate war itself. But is there any likelihood of war's being eliminated from human society?

I don't think that one country will maintain exclusive control over nuclear energy forever. I imagine that many countries will eventually come to utilize this power. Recently newspaper reports have said that the Soviet Union has successfully produced an atomic bomb and that a large uranium ore deposit was discovered in Australia. If these stories are true, then the annihilation not only of specific nations, but of all humanity, becomes a very real threat. As President Truman is said to have pointed out during a guest lecture at an American university, unless a rapport based on tolerance, understanding, wisdom and consideration can be established among the nations of the world, we will certainly engage in nuclear warfare again.

But when will we ever achieve such a rapport? Lately I've begun to wonder if our modern scientific age augurs our future happiness or eventual self-destruction. I often speculate on whether mankind is not now propelling the earth—which evolved through the age of trilobites in the Paleozoic period, reptiles in the Mesozoic era and gigantic animals in the Cenozoic period—toward an era which will be populated by new forms of life.

The United Nations, which was formally established last October, soon after our surrender, is now attempting to provide some answers to problems posed by the development and use of the atomic bomb. It oversees both a special commission on nuclear energy and the United Nations Security Council. An agency called UNESCO (United Nations Educational, Scientific, and Cultural Organization) has also been established. I am hoping that the UN will offer some thoughtful answers.

Japan however has not yet become a member of either the United Nations or UNESCO. In fact, Japan has not yet been given the option of joining these organizations.

But thanks to the unexpectedly extensive protection and benevolent guidance of the United States, the strongest of the Allied powers, the people of Japan no longer need to fear for their safety. We now enjoy many of the basic necessities of life, and have acquired a spiritual composure we did not have during the war.

The most immediate problems posed for Japan by the advent of the atomic bomb are the innumerable practical matters requiring immediate attention. I must discuss a few of them with you here since they concern the welfare of our three children.

About last November, an item in the newspaper quoted Foreign Minister Eden of England as having said that the atomic bomb rendered all previous concepts of sovereignty meaningless. Those words apply most literally to the developments taking place in Japan. As you well know, Japan has been under the reign since ancient times of an "unbroken line" of emperors who have been venerated as divine. But this January the current emperor, acting of his own accord, publicly repudiated all claims to divinity and declared that he was a mere human being. You would have been astounded. What is more, a new constitution is now being drawn up, under which the emperor's absolute sovereignty will be replaced by sovereignty of the people. Imperial Japan is being reborn as a democratic country.

Japan has renounced war, so it no longer possesses any armed forces whatsoever and of course the militarists have been purged from government. Suddenly we are free of the repressive bonds of feudalism. When you think about it, Japan was ruled for centuries by emperors and aristocratic classes. Various military cliques have also held power since the twelfth century up through World War II: a period of more than seven hundred years.

As you know, Japan was roused from its isolation in the mid-nineteenth century by Commodore Perry of the United States and compelled to open its doors to world commerce and trade. This was followed of course by the Meiji Restoration of 1868, in which Japan managed to acquire the trappings of a modern constitutional state. But directly beneath this veneer, the Japanese people were still subject to the absolute authority of emperor and aristocracy. Somewhere along the line, the traditional aristocracy was replaced by a modern substitute—the huge *zaibatsu* financial cliques which were dissolved by the Allied powers soon after the surrender. It only becomes clear now that we were cleverly manipulated and exploited all along by the *zaibatsu* and by the military with its promotion of adulation of the emperor as Supreme Commander.

To protect this dual authority structure, the sanctity of the family system was held to be inviolable, and people were compelled to live their lives within the bounds of its restrictive tenets. Laws, social mores, moral codes and cultural and educational policies were established on the basis of this system. The family was proudly extolled as being at the heart of a nation composed of united families and unique in its reign by an unbroken line of emperors from time immemorial. But this overemphasis on the family led to many abuses. Vesting the head of the family with absolute familial authority led to the suppression of a great deal of individual freedom. You and I experienced all kinds of difficulties over just these points. You suffered because you were so naive, honest and unprotesting while I, on the other hand, though not unaware of the system's injustices, rationalized them as being "the way things were."

But with the development and use of this new weapon, Japan surrendered to and was occupied by the Allied powers. Under the directives and guidance of these powers the citizens of Japan were finally freed from the control of the financial and military authorities and rescued from the tradition of overvaluing the family system. People now laud these changes as marking the arrival of an age of democracy and humanism. Some go so far as to boast that this has been a "bloodless" revolution, which could hardly be further from the truth.

Limiting ourselves to the islands of Japan, an appalling amount of blood was shed. Before the "revolution" could get underway, 260,000 people were killed and 420,000 were wounded.

In fact, the word "revolution" is completely misleading, since this is not a revolution that was started by the will of the people but one that was generated by the Allied powers, particularly the United States. What is happening is that Japan is taking its first faltering steps under the tutelage of the United States.

The problem confronting me at the moment is the question of how I should bring up and educate our three young children so that they can lead fulfilling lives and take the best possible advantage of this new age of democracy and humanism. As a start I enrolled all three of them at a boarding school that opened last November. I thought that this would free me from the daily chore of having to prepare meals for them and would prepare them for life in a dramatically changed social environment. But it didn't work out quite as I had planned.

For example, I had a hard time obtaining extra foodstuffs for the children. Meals themselves were not a problem, as these were supplied by the school. What I was worried about was providing the children with something to enjoy between meals. The school officials had told parents that they were free to bring treats for their children, within "reasonable" limits, but they didn't indicate what they meant by "reasonable," nor did they apparently take into consideration the shortage of anything clearly reasonable on the market at that time. When I visited the children, taking what little I had been able to gather, I noticed that their classmates were being supplied by their parents with large quantities of expensive items. Although our children never directly mentioned the vast difference in what I gave them and what some of their classmates were receiving, I felt guilty and miserable. I worried that our children's personalities would eventually become warped in such an environment. Both the parents and teachers of the children showed exactly the kind of egoistic attitude toward family that I had come to deplore.

Other regulations were ignored as well. For instance, visits were to be limited to one per month, and overnight stays were forbidden. I had followed these rule to the letter but then the children started asking me why I didn't visit more often and pleaded that I stay overnight when I come. The regulations were posted in large letters at the entry to the dormitory. I pointed this out and told them that we must abide by the rules, whereupon Kazuko gave a thin smile and said that nobody else really did. I was dumbfounded. She said some parents visited their children every three days, and that quite a few stayed overnight, some of them sleeping beside their children. I felt as if I had been struck hard on the head. Even in the schools there is yet no sense of social responsibility.

My greatest fear was that the children's mental growth might be affected by the material and spiritual deprivation they were experiencing and that as a result they might become delinquent. I had seen too many delinquent, deprived children—products of the ravages of war—wandering the streets of Hiroshima, Osaka and other cities. I saw an international edition of a Chinese newspaper that carried a large headline reading, "Report to the Homeland—Vagrant Children a New Problem for a Defeated Japan." The streets were so overrun with such children that the topic was considered newsworthy for readers in China. Many children are still in this situation now.

You can imagine how I felt when faced with the stark reality of prevailing social conditions and the circumstances under which our children lived at the school dormitory. But what could I, a down-and-out victim of the war with three children to look after, do about such things?

A few months ago, I urgently needed to find a girls' high school for Kazuko. This was hard enough, but a bigger problem was that Keiichi and Kinji would be left by themselves in the school dormitory when Kazuko went off to another school. I had been in poor health for some time and so was at my wits' end. At just about that time, my former student, Miss Ono, suddenly came to visit. She had heard, she said, of the difficulties I was having. No sooner had I told her a little bit about our situation than she said, "Let me look after the children for you. Actually, that's what I came about." I was taken aback. But on reflection I realized what a kind and timely offer it was. I think you know that she was still single and living with her mother. I decided to entrust the children to their care from the beginning of April. Kazuko entered the school where Miss Ono works while Keiichi and Kinji transferred to the primary school in the village where the Onos live.* I'm now alone in this storehouse.

I visit the children now and again. They have become true

---

* [The author and Miss Ono eventually married, and continued from that point to raise the children together.]

village children and are enjoying a healthy, carefree life.

As for me, I have lost all the faith I once had in Japan and Japanese people. My experiences living in a defeated nation over the past year have only reinforced this feeling for me. I heard from a newspaper reporter that one navy admiral said shortly after the surrender that, "Japan's defeat arose not only from the difference in capability of the two countries, but from the difference in the capability of the average Japanese versus the average American." I think he's right.

Today, a student who was a navy reserve cadet visited the university and said that a young officer told his group, just before it was demobilized, that unconditional surrender was inevitable after such a disastrous defeat. The officer said that we all needed to relearn everything from scratch from the Americans. Again, I agree completely.

Japanese can be compared to small children at a field athletic meet cheering on contestants who are running neck and neck, without realizing that the top runner has already lapped the others three or four times. We must strip ourselves of false pride and learn all we can about this "top runner": his running strategy, the food he eats, his mode of living, everything. I think this is the most pressing task for us. We must strive to be people worthy of respect; everything we do must be based on this premise.

You remember how I used to recite to you the poem "Netsuke Country" by Kotaro Takamura.

> *Prominent cheekbones, thick lips, slanting eyes,*
> *With a countenance like that of a netsuke figurine*
> *Carved by the master Sangoro.*
> *Face blank, as if devoid of soul,*
> *No sense of self, anxious about trivia,*
> *Cheapening life, vain, brittle and small, yet*
> *Self-satisfied.*
> *Like monkeys, like foxes, like flying squirrels,*
> *Like gobyfishes, like killifishes, like ogre-faced ridge-end tiles,*

like shards of chinaware. Such are the Japanese.

Until now, Japanese have indeed been as Takamura caricatures them here. But even Takamura, his admiration of the mystic and pacifist French writer Rolland notwithstanding, was a member of an organization that cooperated in the war effort. He also participated in, or was made to participate in, the Association Supporting Imperial Rule.

Last winter I trudged through deep snow to visit him in the remote mountain cabin in Iwate Prefecture where he has isolated himself since the war in a form of penance for his pro-war activities. While we talked, I came around to believing that defeat was Japan's inevitable destiny.

"I will certainly apologize, if need be," Takamura said.

In his poem "Things Depressing" he says:

> *Trying to justify oneself for the rest of one's life,*
> *That is somewhat despicable,*
> *That is somewhat depressing.*

This poem touches me to the quick. Justifying ourselves is what Japanese history has done all along—and what our work as historians has entailed. Very few historians—even those with a strong commitment to academic excellence—were altogether free of the propensity to justify Japan's past actions. I was one of many who engaged in this despicable form of self-deceit. It is time for me to learn from scratch again.

This April, when I stood at the lectern for the first time since the surrender, I apologized to my students from the bottom of my heart. I had by then decided to step down and had in fact handed in my resignation to Professor Kurita, the head of our department. I have since stayed on in Hiroshima, attending to affairs concerning the children and making various preparations for a new life. Meanwhile, the children are in safe hands and my preparations are almost complete. I probably won't be here by August 19, the first anniversary of your death. I will let you know, in due course, how my new life turns out.*

I am looking forward with great expectations to a life free of mental and physical encumbrances so that I can begin to make amends for the consequences of my past self-deception. I will try to live the rest of my life as I've always wished to: with complete abandon, in the manner of Walt Whitman, whom I so admire.

This is the only way I know to respond to the mute lesson of our city's "thinker," who seems to be warning people of every nation, including the Japanese, not to perpetrate another Hiroshima. I don't know about anyone else. But this is the way that I'll go.

—*August 6, 1946*

---

* [The author had hoped to leave teaching and become a Buddhist priest; however, university officials convinced him to stay on.]

Appendices

The Author's Letter to the Children

Dearest Kazuko and Keiichi,
It seems that the two of you are doing well and are getting used to your new life. I am always so happy to receive your letters. Today too I am writing this letter to both of you.

It's been one week but your mother has not yet returned. I understand that she's working with the people of the village to help build air-raid shelters in the mountains in Jigozen. I am sure it must be very hard work. I keep thinking that she will come back—all worn out—any time now, and I even went to the station to check, but she had not come yet. Surely she will arrive today, although I do worry about whether or not she will be able to get a train ticket.

So your father has been very busy all by himself: cooking meals, getting things packed up to send, seeing visitors, writing letters ... I arranged to have Mr. Inomata hold onto the boxes of your books. And Mr. Utsumi (who sometimes comes to the Miyazawa circle meetings) said his daughter and son would take care of your Girls' Day and Boys' Day dolls. He's coming to get them tomorrow so I will set them up and enjoy one last day with them today.

Some other people from the Miyazawa circle are going to look after the rest of our other boxes till the war is over, which means I will not have to bring very much with me to Hiroshima.*

---

* [The author was teaching in Himeji through the spring of 1945, when a transfer brought him and his family to Hiroshima.]

176

This way we can cut down on the possessions we have to worry about, and no matter where each of us is we can be ready to help fight for our country.

Today we have a meeting of the Miyazawa circle. I hope you two will not forget about him. I hope that you'll do the *kamishibai* storyboard drama for your friends there and tell them all about Kenji. In any case, be sure not to forget the poem "Standing Up to the Rain" and always try, wherever you might be, to live by it.*

Today we've had so many air-raid alerts, I've been in and out all day. The people in charge of the alerts must be extremely busy. The war just keeps on getting worse. The five of us are now all completely split up and we must realize that we cannot know which of us may be killed first. We must try to do whatever we can to help other people, and remember what Kenji said: "don't think of yourself." That is the best way we can help our country.

Are you keeping your shoes neat and lined up right by the door? No matter where you are, take a minute to do this. If you are careful in little things, the bigger things in life will be easy too. Be sure to be yourselves. Just do whatever you yourselves believe to be right.

Yesterday I got the letters from the two of you (even though Kazuko's was addressed to Mother) and I ran around frantically trying to find all the things you asked for. With your mother away, and me trying to pack things up, it was difficult. You should have seen me, like the owner of Kenji's "restaurant of many orders." Somehow I managed by the evening to find all the things you had asked for. Anything else that you still need, I will send later. The washbasins must have arrived by now.

The two of you are accumulating a lot of things there now, so be sure to keep them neat. You know we always had to tell you how bad you were at keeping things neat. Your mother and I are both worried about you being on your own.

You must put your things away neatly, and keep a list of what you have. I am sure it must be difficult, since you have so few storage

---

* [See page 193.]

boxes, but the war is only going to get worse from this point, and you must be able to live out of a single box.

What if the enemy should suddenly arrive, and you have no idea where any of your own things are? You must—you absolutely must—keep your things neat.

I plan to get to Hiroshima in about May, and when I do I will send you a telegram. After that time, you should address your letters to me "care of Mr. Tetsuji Tanaka."

Yesterday I sent the things you asked for, in separate packages to each of you. Be sure to take the paper and string off the packages and put these away carefully. Do not waste anything.

Japan is at war, so it is not easy to get any new pencils or paper or notebooks or other things you may need. Treat your things with care and be sure not to lose them. That will be one thing you can do to help fight for your country.

Please let me know anything else you need. Don't try to keep your list small, but just tell me everything you need. I've made a list of what we've sent so far. Please check it over carefully.

Kazuko, you had an Eighth-Level Language Book here, didn't you? It isn't here now. I sent a pair of underwear that I found. I looked all over for a bar of laundry soap but I couldn't find one so I just sent the one we had been using here. When your mother comes back she'll send you a new one. I didn't know where your *geta* straps or *zori* sandals were, so I was not able to send them. We'll send them later.

Keiichi, with your mother away, I wasn't sure about the needle and thread. I could find only one needle. I'll send more later. I didn't know what kind of science notebook you needed either, so I just sent a regular notebook. Please use it for now.

I sent each of you a wicker-style bamboo box. I also sent paper bags. Please use these to organize your things.

We have almost no stamps or postcards. I sent a few stamps. The postcards I sent are the kind that you need to put stamps on. Be careful.

If you run out of stamps, take the letter or the postcard to the post office. You can just pay them five *sen* for a postcard or ten *sen* for a letter and they will send it for you. Ask your teacher, and do this if you run out of stamps.

On your last letter, Kazuko, you put only a five-*sen* stamp. Be careful. And in your letter, Keiichi, I noticed that you got a lot of characters wrong, so you be careful too.

Where you are, in the mountains, it's cooler than in Himeji or Hiroshima, so be sure to stay warm. Keep yourselves strong and healthy so you can help Japan fight the war.

Kinji is going off to school every day now from Grandpa Tanaka's. I told him that if he wasn't good we'd ship him right back to Himeji to school by himself. He said he'd rather stay in Hiroshima.

How about writing to him to cheer him up?

You both are living in a beautiful part of the country with kind people who are taking good care of you, and you have good food to eat. Always remember to be grateful for these things.

April 21, 1945

Father

THINGS SENT

(Items sent earlier to both of you)
  1. Washbasins (1 for each)
  2. A drawing notebook (1 for each)
  3. *Kamishibai* storyboard dramas (1 for each)

Things sent yesterday (to both of you)
  1. A wicker-style bamboo box (1 for each)
  2. Books (2 or 3 for each)
  3. Paper bags (2 or 3 for each)
  4. W*ashi* calligraphy paper
  5. Manuscript paper
  6. Pencils and erasers (2 of each for both of you)

7. Notebooks (1 for each)
8. Envelopes and stationery (for letter writing)
9. Stamps (in a bag)
10. Picture postcards and blank postcards
11. Cup
12. Colored ink decals

Things I sent only to Kazuko

1. Laundry soap (I will send more later)
2. Shampoo (wash your hair before it gets smelly)
3. *Geta* clogs (I wasn't sure, so I sent an old pair. We will have to send *geta* straps and *zori* sandals later).
4. One pair of underwear (we will send more later)

Things I sent only to Keiichi

1. Needle and thread (your mother will send more later)
2. Science notebook (you will have to make do with a regular notebook)
3. Music notebook
4. One box of pastel crayons
5. One pair of *zori* sandals
6. One belly band and one pair of underwear

Fumiyo's Letter to the Children

Kazuko-chan,

I received the photographs of the "smiling squad" at ten o'clock on the morning of the sixth. Everybody in it is certainly smiling, smiling, smiling. You know what I started doing when I saw the pictures? Smile, smile, smile!

Kazuko, I see that your pockets are bulging as usual. What on earth could have gotten into them? If you go around with so many things in your pockets, it will tire you out. You might want to try carrying a tiny bit less!

How are the indigo *monpe* pants? If they're comfortable, I'll make you another pair. How are my Number One Girl's bloomers holding up? I'd like to make you some more but the material is over at Uncle Tetsuji and Aunt Mieko's, so when I go to Hiroshima I'll get it and make some up and send them right away. Wait a little longer. How are the shirts?

Kinji will be coming with me to see you next time (we're planning on about the twentieth). I hope to bring you some summer futons and other things. For instance, roasted barley flour. I'm sure it is nothing new to your classmates, but if you think that they would like some I will be happy to bring it. Have the six pairs of *zori* sandals arrived yet? About the cloth for your needlework class—when you think you might be needing some more, let me know in advance, since I will need some time to get it.

Out here in the countryside, it is one volunteer project after another, day in and day out. It keeps us very busy.

Everybody is fine at Aunt Setsuko's, including Grandma. There are lots of tomatoes in the garden. If they are ripe by the next time I visit, I'll bring some with me. I know you'll like them!

Father is now at the Miyazawas' in Iwate Prefecture. He's fine. Let's all be strong and keep our spirits up.

Kinji has finally written a letter to you. Be sure not to laugh at him, but encourage him. That will make him happy, and he will want to write again.

Your teachers are well too, I see. Try not to be a bother to them, but to do everything you can by yourself.

When I see Nagata-sensei next, I want to thank her for everything she's done.

Take good care of yourself.

Mother

Kinji's Composition

The morning of August 6, I was playing in front of Uncle Tetsuji and Aunt Mieko's house. Someone yelled that some B-29 bombers had come. I started to run toward the house to go into the air-raid shelter. Just then I thought there was a flash, like lightning. After that I don't know what happened.

When I woke up, I felt something heavy on me and I saw a beam of bright sunlight coming from over my head. I thought I was killed by a bomb. I was crying and yelling for my mother. But every time I moved my head, something like sand started pouring down my chest. I heard somebody say "Help! Help!" So I stopped crying and said "Help! Help!" too, over and over. Then a voice up above me said, "Hold on, we'll get you out." I think it was the soldier who was staying upstairs at Aunt Mieko's. I kept yelling and tried to move my arms and legs. I could move them a little. Soon the weight that was pressing on me got lighter. Sand was pouring down my neck. It got brighter and I felt somebody put his hands under my arms and pull on me. It was the soldier from Aunt Mieko's.

After he pulled me out, I looked around. Aunt Mieko's and our house were totally destroyed. I had been trapped under the wall of their house. One of my shoes was gone and I couldn't find it.

Aunt Mieko was standing there with the baby, Kan-chan, in her arms. "You were lucky, Kinji," she said. Her shoulder was bleeding. There was blood on my shirt too, around my stomach. But it didn't hurt.

All of a sudden the house next door started burning. Soon Aunt

Mieko's house and our house started burning too. I saw my school jacket and my bag inside the house. I wanted to go get them but Aunt Mieko wouldn't let me. She said it was dangerous. I saw that goldfish swimming around in the tank in front of our house.

Aunt Mieko and me ran to Funairi Hospital. Grandpa Tanaka came out of the hospital. It was totally destroyed. The four of us got on a boat that was tied up at the dock near the hospital. There were plenty of other people already on the boat. Some were bleeding all over. The hospital and the houses on the riverbank started burning and it got so hot even on the boat that I thought we were all going to burn to death. Aunt Mieko grabbed the baby and me and got in the water and pulled us over to a sandbar.

There were lots of people already on the sandbar. Suddenly it started to rain. The rain was real black. My shirt got all spotted black but the rain didn't put the fire out.

After a while, Uncle Tetsuji came along on his bicycle, looking for us. "Let's go to Aunt Setsuko's in Jigozen," he said, and he strapped the baby onto his back. He said he would come back for me next and told us to keep walking slow. He went up the riverbank and rode away.

Aunt Mieko, Grandpa Tanaka and I went up the riverbank too and started walking. It was hot from the fires. We crossed Kan'on Bridge and walked across some vegetable fields. We came to another river but there was no bridge. People were walking across the river so we started to too. The water got deeper and soon it was up to my neck. I was scared of the water. A man said he would carry me. He lifted me up and carried me.

When we got across, we looked at Hiroshima. It was horrible. It was covered with black smoke and red flames. We went through some vegetable fields, crossed a streetcar bridge and came to a wide road. "This is the tourist road," Aunt Mieko said. I was glad because I knew the tourist road went to Jigozen. I wanted to get to Jigozen soon because I thought Mother was there waiting for me.

One of my feet was bare and the road was hot. It was full of broken glass too. It pricked when I walked on it, but not so bad. There were lots of other people there walking to Jigozen too. Almost all of them were barefoot too.

When we got to Inokuchi some men gave us bread. I like bread but I didn't feel like eating it then.

A train was waiting and they were letting everybody on it for free. We got on too. It was full. The train stopped at Hatsukaichi. There was a girl about my age in the station, yelling "Mommy! Mommy!" It made me feel bad.

We started walking again. I know how to get from Hatsukaichi to Jigozen. I walked fast and was the leader. When I got to Aunt Setsuko's house, I yelled "Mommy!" But Aunt Setsuko came out instead. Mother had not arrived yet.

Aunt Setsuko put some medicine on my cuts and a white bandage on my stomach. She gave me a glass of water and told me to go to sleep. I lay down beside Kan-chan and fell asleep. When I got up, it was night but Mother had still not come.

Kazuko's Letter to Her Family

Dear Father,

How are you? I drew this map today. See where I wrote "Hexagon Head" next to that face? That's our nickname for Okabe-sensei because his head is shaped like a hexagon. Isn't it a funny name? I didn't understand it the first time I heard it. Look how busy the bees are, flying over the hives. In the mountains behind the temple there are lots of the dogtooth violets that Kenji-sama liked. When the flowers bloom I will send you some, and some leaves too. Well, take good care of yourself. Goodbye!

Dear Mother,

How are you? I am great and working hard. I drew this map today. "Hexagon Head" always makes us laugh, he's very funny. Since school started, our class is the only one with a perfect attendance record. How about that! Okabe-sensei is always swaggering around and boasting about it when he sees the other teachers.

In the mountains behind the temple there are lots of dogtooth violets blooming. At the Katohs' house they have a baby horse and when we go there to take a bath we always get dried chestnuts or some other snack. It's really nice. Well, Mother, take good care of yourself. Goodbye!

Dear Kinji,

How are you? I am fine. Are you studying hard? I am too. I drew an interesting picture today. We call Okabe-sensei "Hexagon Head." It's a funny nickname. Well, take care of yourself and be good. Goodbye.

Kazuko

Kazuko's Diary (August 18–19, 1945)

August 18, 1945

I went to school today for the ceremonial reading of the rescript that the emperor issued on the fifteenth, announcing the end of the war. When we arrived, the teacher told us to go over to Renshoji Temple, since the soldiers were using the school's gymnasium, where we were supposed to have the ceremony. So we went to Renshoji, which is gloomy inside—big and dark.

We all stood up when Mr. Nakao, the gym teacher, asked us to, and then listened carefully while the head teacher read the rescript out loud. I cannot imagine just what the emperor may have felt, but I am sure he must have been mortified. When the head teacher finished, we sat down on the tatami and listened to a speech. With tears in his eyes, he told us stories about some of the cruel deeds that the United States and England did. How horrible, I thought. Then I realized we were in exactly the pitiful state that our principal had warned us we would reach if we were to lose the war. There were probably some students there whose family had been killed in the bombing. I felt very sorry for them. The head teacher kept crying. When the Americans, British, Chinese and Russian troops landed, he said, they would not be kind, like Japanese soldiers. There was no doubt that they would be extremely merciless and cruel. I began to think it might have been better if I had been killed. But then I decided to stop thinking that way and resolved to bear any hardships that might be imposed on me. That way, maybe the period of my forced labor would be shorter. Anyway, I must just bear up and be strong, I thought. We went back to our dormitories when the ceremony was over. Then we went to a spot near the Takano railway station to bring back some wooden boards. It was quite far away and my feet hurt but we kept at it. Each of us carried three boards each time. Then we went back to the dormitory for lunch. We were very hungry so it tasted wonderful.

After lunch, I thought I would take a rest. I took out some cushions and lay down for a while. Then a naval officer came in. I stared at him for a few seconds before I realized that it was Uncle Shiro. He told me that he had come to get me because my mother's condition had gotten a little worse. So I got some things together quickly and rushed around notifying my teachers. Then we left right away. I kept worrying about Mother's condition. We brought a letter from the dormitory addressed to the evacuation headquarters, which is near the large bridge, but no one was there when we stopped so Uncle Shiro went to get the head teachers. Mr. Nakao came and wrote out a travel certificate for me. It started to rain then, hard and loud, so we were going to wait until it let up, but it didn't look like it was going to, so finally we went outside and resigned ourselves to getting wet. Just then we saw Keiichi coming, and he had an umbrella. We ran over to him and all got under, while Uncle Shiro held it. We stopped at Seiganji Temple to get Keiichi's things. Soon the rain stopped. While we were hurrying to the station, I noticed that Kei-chan had nothing with him except a small parcel wrapped in cloth. When I asked him what was in it, he said it was something that Kinji had asked for. When we got to the station, we found Mrs. Yamanaka there waiting. She and Uncle Shiro talked for quite a long time. The train was more than one hour late. As soon as we got on, I got my handkerchief out and ready. Then when we went past the dormitory I waved it back and forth as hard as I could. The students waved back. The train was not so crowded. A woman with a baby took the seat next to me and gave me some boiled beans. The scenery outside was quite different now than when we first came. The green hills were very beautiful but the entire area from around Kayano Station to Hiroshima had been terribly bombed. Hiroshima Station had been destroyed. We got off and boarded a train bound for Iwakuni but it just sat there for a long time so we thought maybe we should get off and walk to Koi. From there we would be able to take the Miyajima Line to Aunt Setsuko's. But when we asked at the ticket gate, they said that the trains to the suburbs had stopped running for the day. We went back to the train for Iwakuni but while we were waiting for it to leave, a second train came in and we got on that one instead. The view from the window was cruel and terrible. Koi Station was completely flattened. When I turned around in my seat, I saw the mother of my friend, Fujino. Then we got off at Hatsuka-ichi Station and asked if there were any trains running. But there weren't so we walked. We went fast so we got there in less than thirty minutes.

When we stepped onto the porch at Aunt Setsuko's house, Father was standing there waiting for us. His left arm was supported in a piece of white cloth slung around his neck. He said that Mother had gotten hurt when she was outside Fukuya's waiting for a train.

The first time Father told her we were there she said, "What?" but the second time she said, "Oh, they are?" Her face was very thin.

Kei-chan and I sat down on the floor side by side, right up near her head and greeted her.

"Hello, Mother."

She gazed at us for a while without saying anything. Father put his hand on my head and said, "Look, Kazuko is here."

"You've gotten so big," she said. Then Father patted Kei-chan on the head and told Mother, "Keiichi too."

"Oh yes, my little member of the 'smiling squad,'" Mother said. My teachers out in the country always made us smile a lot whenever they took group photographs to send our parents, so in her letters Mother always called my class the "smiling squad." She seemed to have gotten me and Kei-chan mixed up. I looked questioningly at Father. He lifted his hand to his forehead and told us that Mother's high fever had affected her head and that we should keep quiet. I suddenly felt very sad. Aunt Setsuko made dinner for us but I couldn't eat much.

After dinner, Kei-chan and I went back to her room. Kei-chan fanned her face gently while I kept wetting down a hand towel and then squeezing it out and laying it on her forehead and chest. Father was sitting next to her. Kin-chan was grumpy because Kei-chan wouldn't play with him, but pretty soon he lay down beside Mother and fell asleep.

In the meantime Father, who had been checking Mother's pulse, noticed something strange. So he called Aunt Setsuko and Uncle Shiro, and everybody came into the room. Mother opened her eyes wide and said, "What are you doing here? What happened? What do you want?" I couldn't hold back my tears.

Then Father brought out a photo of baby Toshiko and showed it to Mother, asking, "Do you know who this is?"

"It's Toshiko," Mother said clearly.

Then I showed her a picture of Kenji Miyazawa.

She looked at it and said "Kenji-chama," in a baby voice.

Tears started falling from my eyes again. Father's eyes were full of tears too.

Mother went on. "Let's go together into the blue sky. Let's hurry off to Hanamaki. Did you find out yet where Polan Plaza is? Let's hurry and ride on the Milky Way railroad!"

I thought she might be a little better now, because when she saw the photo of Kenji Miyazawa it reminded her of what we used to say about his stories.

But Father said, "She's really lightheaded."

This made me sad again and I tried hard to cool Mother's forehead and chest. Suddenly she opened her eyes and looked right at me, and said in a scolding tone, "It's late. Off to bed." When I realized Mother was worried about us even though she was so sick herself, I started to cry again. I went out in the kitchen to get a fresh bucket of water and then kept on cooling off Mother's forehead and chest. Soon she fell into a calm sleep.

"She seems to be a bit more stable now. Everybody please go and get some rest," Father said.

Aunt Setsuko and Uncle Shiro left and went off to bed. Then Father said to us, "You must be tired. Go to bed now." Kei-chan lay down beside Kin-chan and fell asleep. I stayed up a while longer, but since Father kept insisting, I finally lay down beside Kei-chan. But I couldn't get to sleep at first. I remember hearing the clock strike three.

August 19, 1945

I got up a little after five in the morning to tend to Mother. Soon Masako arrived from Kure to help look after her. So I had breakfast and returned to Mother's bedside. She asked me to open the bottom drawer of the cupboard. I tried, but it was locked.

"It's locked, Mother," I said.

"Is it?" she said with a sad face.

Then she spoke to Father. "There's a can of peaches in the closet. Would you get it?"

Father looked for it but he could only find a can of mandarin oranges. He opened it and said, "She must have gotten these mixed up."

Father gave her some of the juice from the can to drink. Then she said, "Give some to them."

I was so touched. What a kind mother. What a sweet mother. We children had three sections of orange each. The fruit was more delicious than usual, I thought, because she gave it to us. When I gave her some juice she smiled happily. Then she kept on smiling so long, and gazing at me, that I could see something was wrong, as if the fever had gone to her brain. Then I could hardly stand to see her smile that way any more. Father left to take care of something in Itsukaichi and I was very worried about what would happen if Mother got worse while he was gone. Fortunately, he came back before noon.

After lunch I mixed up some orange juice, sugared water and honey and gave it to her. She gulped it down quickly. Uncle Hideichi came from Kanayacho and brought us some grapes. We squeezed the juice out of them and gave it to Mother. She liked it too and drank a lot of it. A little while later, I was startled to see something that looked like a piece of thick string come out of her mouth. It was a big roundworm.

After dinner I went to her bedside. Her eyes had sunk deep down into their sockets and she was having trouble breathing. I was told that she had vomited blood. I never left her bedside after that.

"Fumiyo! Fumiyo!" Father cried.

"What a noisy father!" Mother grumbled. "You children are lucky to have such an amusing father." A minute later she said, "Where have Kazuko and the others gotten off to?"

After that she seemed to have even more difficulty breathing, and the intervals between her breaths got longer. We realized the end was approaching. At eight-thirty that evening, she drew in a large breath and left this world. I cried out, loudly. Losing one's only mother is a sorrow that cannot be expressed in writing or in words.

Our cries of "Mother! Mother!" were answered only by forlorn echoes. Our kind, gentle mother would never return to us.

She passed away with a photograph of our departed baby sister, Toshiko, and another one of Kenji Miyazawa, on her breast. She was probably riding on Kenji-sama's Milky Way railroad now. Father, Kei-chan, Kinji and I cleaned her body. It was still warm. There was a very big blister at her hip from a burn. It was red and must have been very painful. We dressed her in her favorite kimono and scattered paper flower petals over her breast.

We braided her hair and she looked like a young girl. She had died in great agony, so we had difficulty closing her eyes and mouth. Her eyes would open again, even after we had closed them. I never dreamed that our beloved mother would die such a horrible death at the hands of the Americans. It all seemed like a bad dream. If only it were a dream, I thought. I couldn't help feeling that I had caused Mother's death. None of this would have happened if she had not gone to buy me the ointment.

I put another kimono over her feet. Smoke from the sticks of incense wafted through the air near her head. Father recited some Buddhist sutras, praying for Mother's happiness in the next world. We laid mattresses on either side of her body and I took the one right next to her. I couldn't stop crying when I realized that this would be the last time I would sleep beside her—my kind mother who had smiled into my eyes just a little while ago. Oh mother, my mother!

Standing Up to the Rain
—Kenji Miyazawa

Standing up to the rain,
Standing up to the wind,
Stand up to snow and summer heat.
Be strong of body
And don't be greedy.
Never get mad,
But always have a smile on your face.
Eat four *go* of brown rice a day
With some miso and a few vegetables.
No matter what, don't think of yourself,
Listen carefully and try to understand,
And don't forget.
In the shade of a grove of pine trees on a plain
Live in a small thatched hut.
If a child is sick in the East,
Go and look after that child.
If a Mother is tired in the West,
Go and carry her bundles of rice.
If someone is about to die in the South,
Go and say there is nothing to be afraid of.
If people are disputing and litigating in the North,
Go and tell them to stop, it's below them.
Shed tears when crops suffer from drought,
Be beside yourself with worry when it's cold in summer.
Be called a good-for-nothing by everyone,
Don't be praised, but don't be a burden.
This is the kind of person
I would like to be.

Afterword

I began reading Toyofumi Ogura's *Letters from the End of the World* in the dim glow of a small lamp. When I finished, I was fully transplanted from my little shack, nestled in the tranquil mountains, to a world of smoldering debris. I read the book again the next night and then, later, several more times. I was deeply moved each time by the force of Mr. Ogura's narrative. He recounts his experiences from beginning to end in a simple and unsophisticated style. The ghastliness of what he first thought was the blowing up of a munitions depot and then slowly realized was in fact the world's first experience of an atomic bomb sent cold shivers down my spine. I could hardly bring myself to re-read his account of his wife's suffering and death from radiation sickness.

The book brought home to me just how hopeless mankind's condition is if the loss of these vast numbers of people fails to warn us how we must turn toward peace.

Any politician or member of the military who reads this account will surely lose all taste for warfare. Unless future conflicts are resolved before people take up arms, the sacrifice at Hiroshima will have been in vain. I hope people around the world will gain from this book a more intimate sense of the unbearable tragedy of nuclear warfare.

Kotaro Takamura
February 1949

The author's daughter Kazuko, who was eleven years old at the time of the bombing, is shown here in 2001, at age sixty-seven. She worked for nearly forty years teaching language and literature in junior high and high schools. Since her retirement, she has been doing volunteer work with both senior citizens and children. She has a daughter of her own, who is in her thirties and cares for children in a day-care center.

Glossary

atomic desert: A wasteland created by the dropping of an atomic bomb.

It was widely held, after the bombing of Hiroshima, that the city might become such a desert, and that no plants would be able to grow in the local soil for seventy years. In fact, however, plants began to grow within a few months.

black rain: Precipitation that is a mixture of radioactive debris and rain.

This rain fell heavily for about an hour over a wide area, after the bombing of Hiroshima, spreading radioactive fallout to the northwest part of the city.

censorship: Starting in 1945, the American Occupation forces implemented policies of censorship, under which publications, newspapers, radio programs, movies, dramas and even telephone conversations were to be checked by the army forces for "anti-democratic expressions." These policies, which remained in effect for several years, also forbade writers to take up certain themes, including, for example, loyalty or revenge.

demobilized personnel: Troops discharged from military service.

half-life: The time required for half of the atoms of a given quantity of a radioactive substance to disintegrate. Half-lives vary greatly from one element to another. They can be as short as a fraction of a second or as long as several million years.

hypocenter: The point on the earth's surface that lies directly below the center of a nuclear explosion.

incendiary bombs: Also known as "fire bombs." Used in air raids, they are dropped on targets in order to set fires, rather than produce explosions. The fires are set when the bomb bursts and the incendiary agent it contains is released. In World War II, fire bombs dropped on Japanese cities usually contained jellied petrochemicals such as napalm.

Miyazawa, Kenji: (1896–1933): Poet and author of children's stories. He was a gifted and prolific writer, and one acutely sensitive to the land and to the plight of peasants in the impoverished farming communities in his native Iwate Prefecture, in northern Japan. His poetry celebrates and observes nature while recording the difficulties and triumphs of his spiritual life. His best known children's story is "Ginga tetsudo no yoru" (1927; translated as "Night Train to the Stars," 1987).

Occupation: The period of military and political control of Japan by the United States and its allies following World War II, from 1945 through 1952. During the first years of this period, sweeping political, social and economic reforms were pressed on Japan by the United States. Later the focus turned to planning for Japan's economic rehabilitation and postwar security requirements.

Potsdam Declaration: Declaration issued by the Allies on July 26, 1945, calling on Japan to surrender unconditionally or face utter destruction. The atomic bomb was not actually mentioned in the declaration, however.

radiation sickness: Harmful effect on body tissues caused by exposure to radioactive substances. The actual biological processes involved in this sickness are not well understood, but it is believed that cells become ionized, and that this alters the way they behave. Radiation sickness can occur from exposure to a single massive source of radiation such as an atomic blast, or from repeated exposure to small doses in a plant or laboratory.

The term "radiation sickness" is usually used to refer to "acute radiation sickness," a disease that appears within four months of exposure. Symptoms include nausea, vomiting, diarrhea, delirium, hair loss, erythema, hemorrhaging, bone marrow suppression, and a breakdown of the immune system.

Exposure to radiation can also cause long-term effects which will not be immediately detectable. These can include lowering of red and white blood cell counts, damage to reproductive organs, and increased risk of cancer or genetic damage.

Sino-Japanese War: War between Japan and China fought from August 1, 1894 through April 17, 1895. Japan won easily and overwhelmingly. The war is a landmark in modern Asian international relations because it marked the start of Japan's efforts to industrialize, as well as its territorial expansion and exploitation of other Asian countries.

Takamura, Kotaro: Poet and great admirer of the work of Kenji Miyazawa. During World War II he worked for the government in the war effort; after Japan's defeat, he spent seven years living in an isolated cabin in Iwate Prefecture, where he eventually wrote "Reverence," an indirect apologia for his wartime conduct.

zaibatsu: Financial cliques; industrial conglomerates. Zaibatsu were family-owned holding companies centered around a bank or trading company. The four largest were Mitsui, Mitsubishi, Sumitomo and Yasuda. The zaibatsu played a major role in the Japanese economy from the late 1800s through World War II. They were officially dissolved during the Occupation, as part of an effort to democratize Japanese industry. But after several years, corporate groupings reemerged, on an unofficial basis, along the same lines, and today's big corporate groupings are often viewed as the direct successors to the zaibatsu.

（普及版）英文版 絶後の記録
Letters from the End of the World / TP

2001 年 7 月　第 1 刷発行
2006 年 6 月　第 2 刷発行

著　者　小倉豊文

訳　者　藤井 滋
　　　　村上喜三郎

発行者　富田 充
発行所　講談社インターナショナル株式会社
　　　　〒 112-8652 東京都文京区音羽 1-17-14
　　　　電話　03-3944-6493（編集部）
　　　　　　　03-3944-6492（マーケティング部・業務部）
　　　　ホームページ　www.kodansha-intl.com

印刷所　株式会社 平河工業社
製本所　大日本印刷株式会社